BATHROOMS

BATHROOMS

BY CHRIS CASSON MADDEN

Photographs by John Vaughan

Research Assistance by Kevin Clark and Julie Maher

CLARKSON POTTER/PUBLISHERS
NEW YORK

In memory of John Vaughan, Patty Casson,

Franck Dupont, and Cody—absent friends who are missed and loved

All of the photographs in this book are by John Vaughan except for the following:
Jennifer Levy: pages 92–95
Steve Pierson: pages 5 (below), 89–91
Tim Street-Porter: 99–103, 131–35, 138–41, 164–67, 192, 196
Max Wolfe Sturman: 96–97

Published by Clarkson N. Potter, Inc.,
201 East 50th Street, New York, New York 10022.
Member of the Crown Publishing Group.

Random House, Inc. New York, Toronto, London, Sydney, Auckland
http://www.randomhouse.com/

CLARKSON N. POTTER, POTTER, and colophon
are trademarks of Clarkson N. Potter, Inc.

Manufactured in China

Design by Margaret Hinders

Library of Congress Cataloging-in-Publication Data
  Madden, Chris Casson.
   Bathrooms / by Chris Casson Madden.
   Includes index.
   1. Bathrooms.   2. Interior decoration.   I. Title.
NK2117.B33M33   1996
747.7'8—dc20   95-12991

ISBN 0-517-59938-4

10   9   8

Contents

Introduction

After a decade of living with our ninety-five-year-old master bath, I felt I was ready to take the plunge. I was ready to renovate. After all, my husband Kevin and I had, with relatively few headaches, renovated our kitchen. If nothing else, we had learned that the best way—in fact, I believe the only way—to approach any renovation is just to dig in and do as much research as possible, as far in advance as possible. I could certainly do that.

Although we do have more bathrooms in our home today than I did in the house I grew up in (with a family of eleven, we would line up outside the bathroom to brush our teeth before school),

FOOTBATH

our original master bath was very much of the pre–World War I genre—small and not built for comfort. In fact, to be generous, it was teeny to a fault, linked to our bedroom by a cramped dressing room. If I had one requisite in mind when I began this project, it was to be able to lie in the bath of my dreams in the evenings and gaze out at the moon and the stars. That was number one on my wish list. My husband, on the other hand, had more pressing needs, such as a shower with a built-in mirrored shaving niche and plenty of shelf space. And, of course, efficiency combined with a sense of timelessness was paramount since, although time might be suspended for me during my evening bath, time was of the utmost importance in the morning, with both of us racing out the door.

And so I did my year of research: dreaming, clipping ideas out of magazines, talking to craftspeople and merchants, and pricing fixtures. Yet I wasn't quite sure how to prioritize all of our needs. Enter Zoltan Horvath. Zoltan, a contractor of the first order, not only listened to our dreams and needs, but came up with a few of his own. Why not take down the door between our bathroom and the minuscule dressing area? We would end up with room for a dressing table, and have the three original windows along one wall, enabling the moon to shine in on the tub and me to realize my dream of gazing back at the moon. And seemingly out of nowhere, but with canny and creative maneuvering, he found enough room to install a small marble seat and steam jet spigots in our glassed-in shower, creating a roomy steam bath.

Pale travertine marble now lines the floor and tub, providing a neutral back-drop for what I consider the perfect color in this room—white. Pure white is found throughout: candles, thick thirsty towels, small area rugs, fixtures, toothbrush and cup holders, and, of course, my bar of Ivory. Old black-and-white photographs and an always changing array of fresh-cut flowers or ferns complete our master bath.

On my journey throughout the country looking for great bathrooms to feature in this book, I again happily discovered, as I had in working on my kitchen book, memorable designs that were both inspirational and functional. It became clear to me that, as many observers have noted, the bathroom—our private retreat and refuge—has become the "hot"

room of the nineties, what the family room was to the seventies and the kitchen to the eighties.

I also discovered how creative people integrate extraordinary details in designing this very important room. In turn, I hope this material will inspire you and help you to consider how details can make all the difference when renovating or building a bathroom. Heated towel bars, built-in hampers, specially designed makeup areas, and niches in tubs and showers to hold everything from shaving creams to scented candles are among the pleasures offered in an ideal bathroom.

The layout of the bathroom is as important as that of the kitchen since this is a room that will be just as heavily used. One trick, as I hope you'll see from our blueprints of these rooms, is to mentally go through your daily ablutions before installing any fixture. This visualization will help you in organizing and positioning the various elements you need.

There's much more to a successful bath than just an efficient floor plan. Such features as open and hidden storage, lighting, flooring, tiles, and medicine cabinets can make an enormous difference in how you end up using the space. Luckily, manufacturers are helping us in our search for solutions by developing more efficient products, available in both traditional and contemporary designs. Those seeking, for example, the antique look of old pedestal sinks, huge brass "sunflower" showerheads, and toilets with ceiling cisterns need only look to their local bath shops and mail-order plumbing supply companies.

There is an appealing individuality—even a quirkiness—in bathrooms across the country today. Styles and moods can range from the feel of an actor's dressing room in Lynn von Kersting's bathroom, complete with her own Venetian theatrical crowns, to the strong lines of the "Imperial Ofuro" bath in Santa Fe, a direct descendant of the communal baths of Japan. There are meditative retreats, crisp spas, sybaritic pavilions, and manly dens—all options for this one room. No longer are baths the most standardized room of the house; instead, personality extends most emphatically into the space.

To help you discover your own preferences and undertake your bathroom renovation, think of this book as a resource guide. The individual bath portraits, which I hope will inspire you, are offered complete with specifications, manufacturers, architects, even model names. The second part of *Bathrooms* consists of a thorough survey of choices for flooring, cabinetry, lighting, appliances, and accessories. This guide not only will give you an idea of what's out there, but might suggest a new way to use a product that you might not have thought of before. The list is definitely not all-inclusive, but it will let you know what's available, from classic to contemporary. Remember, choice is the great reward for undertaking the work of building or renovating a bathroom.

After exploring all these special bathrooms, you may wonder how it is to come home to my own renovated bathroom. For me, the proof that it really does work is that I now can't keep my children out of my bathroom, and in their own. I take that as a compliment! And when I do get the room to myself for a long, leisurely bath, I realize how much I love—and need—this space, which fulfills my own personal wish list for a dream bathroom.

Architectural

*Design
strategy pervades
these baths*

Pewabic Perfection

The Eldorado apartment house on New York's Central Park West is considered one of the great masterpieces of art deco architecture. In renovating the master bath of their residence there, Caroline and Michel Zaleski, working with the design firm of Johnson & Wanzenberg, sought to recapture many of the architectural and design elements featured in the historical 1929 edifice. Their penthouse bath, with its wraparound terrace, has stunning views of the Hudson River on the west, and of Central Park and the Manhattan skyline on the east.

Designer Jed Johnson and the homeowners were in full agreement on the design direction of the room. "We couldn't find the original tile," recalls Caroline, "but we decided to use tile from Pewabic Pottery in Detroit, which recently became active again as a working pottery."

Pewabic Pottery is known for the iridescent glazes and deep hues of the custom architectural tile and vessels created by its original owners, Mary Chase Perry Stratton and Horace J. Caulkins, at the turn of the century. Although Pewabic came upon hard times and folded in the 1930s, in 1981 it was reopened as a nonprofit company. Today, the Pewabic Society includes not only tile production but also an educational center, a gallery, a museum, and an archive, which provides access to Mary Stratton's notebooks containing recipes for the glazes.

David Garbo, whose difficult task it was to install this special tile according to the exact specifications laid out

Custom tiles from the Pewabic Pottery form a backdrop to elegant sink fixtures from Urban Archaeology in this New York City apartment.

by Johnson, felt that working with such wonderfully handcrafted pieces was truly "a labor of love." Since each tile is handmade, the color variations are tremendous, and their individual placement can make all the difference in a room.

The bath, located just off the master bedroom and dressing room, was completely reconfigured. A French antique porcelain bathtub, which sits squarely—and majestically—in the middle of the room, takes full advantage of the unparalleled views in all directions from this penthouse aerie. A hand-painted Moorish pattern, inspired by Tiffany designs, was stenciled around the tub's perimeter.

Because the room has three exposures, it is flooded with light all day, creating a solarium effect. And at night, the glitter of New York fills the windows and is reflected in the mirrored inserts flanking the niches of this sophisticated bathroom.

ABOVE LEFT: *The bathroom opens onto a terrace overlooking Central Park. A wrought-iron table and chairs look toward Central Park, while inside, a Crane sink, one of a pair in the room, is set into its own built-in niche.*

LEFT: *The owner's wicker après-bath chaise is occupied.*

OPPOSITE: *The bathtub and handcrafted Pewabic-tiled walls, with their subtle shades of green, take center stage. A hand-painted band was added to the antique French porcelain tub.*

DESIGNER: JED JOHNSON

TILE INSTALLER: DAVID GARBO TILE AND
   MARBLE

GARDEN DESIGNER: MADISON COX

FLOOR: PEWABIC POTTERY

WALLS: PEWABIC POTTERY

TUB: ANTIQUE FRENCH PORCELAIN

SINK PAIR: URBAN ARCHAEOLOGY,
   CRANE

LIGHTING: CUSTOM

TUB/SHOWER FITTINGS: CUSTOM

SINK FIXTURES: URBAN ARCHAEOLOGY

TOILET TISSUE HOLDER: BALDWIN BRASS

TOWELS: PORTICO BED AND BATH

WASTEBASKET: CUSTOM

WICKER CHAIR: THE WICKER GARDEN

OTTOMAN: THE WICKER GARDEN

PLANTERS: KATIE RIDDER

ABOVE LEFT: *The clean lines of the polished nickel toilet paper holder work well with the Pewabic tile.*

BELOW LEFT: *White Pewabic tiles have been interspersed among the green tiles on the floor, breaking up the solid mass. The minimalist toilet provides optimum exposure for the Pewabic tiles.*

ABOVE: *A sculpture in and of itself, a Grueby vase, available through Michael Carey, sits on the sill of the window looking downtown toward midtown Manhattan.*

OPPOSITE: *The tub is strategically placed to take advantage of both the bathroom's east terrace, looking toward Central Park, and its west terrace, which faces the Hudson River. The pattern of the tiles has been cleverly used to zone the different areas of the bath.*

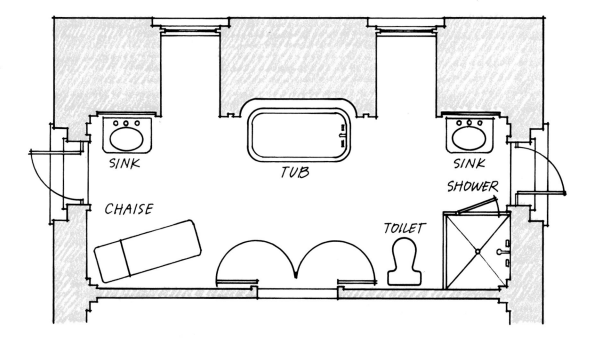

A Modern Aerie

A passion for modern art and Japanese culture provided the inspiration for this bathroom in northern California. The creator of the space, San Francisco designer Arnelle Kase, observes that "simple lines and monochromatic colors serve to create the soothing backdrop for a very Zen environment."

The bathroom addition evolved out of a total renovation of the bedroom wing of the house, which is secluded and surrounded by pine, fir, and eucalyptus. To add light and drama, the ceiling of the bedroom wing was raised and reframed to follow the slope of the roof. A skylight was added to the hall and further improvements to the rest of the house were completed. Located directly off the master bedroom, the master bath is now in the space where a crowded study once existed. Additional square footage and an atrium glass wall in the bath combine to create a more spacious and open feeling.

The addition of the atrium glass introduces substantial natural light and integrates the beauty of the northern

Designer Arnelle Kase used neutral colors to achieve a soothing backdrop for this bathroom. Sink fixtures are by International Faucet Company.

California landscape surrounding the house, creating the ambience that the owners desired. Dimmers on the various lighting fixtures allow for variable uses, from applying makeup to relaxing in the whirlpool with a glass of wine and music in the background.

The focal point of the bathroom is a sycamore and cherry wood center island designed to accommodate all the necessary storage. The glass-top vanity has shallow drawers for makeup; a cabinet above the toilet houses extra tissue and cleaning supplies, and the shower has a built-in bench, in which are stored shampoos and soaps.

Located at the far end of the home and nestled in its striking natural setting, this bath definitely serves as a sensual retreat for the owners.

ARCHITECT: CHERYL CHERNOFF, BARBARA
SCAVULLO DESIGN

DESIGNER: ARNELLE KASE, BARBARA SCAVULLO
DESIGN

GENERAL CONTRACTOR: B. C. LAWSON
CONSTRUCTION

CABINETRY: J. W. SELLARS FURNITURE, CUSTOM

FLOOR: LA FRANCE FRENCH LIMESTONE

WALLS: DUNN EDWARDS

TUB/WHIRLPOOL: PORCHER DELUXE
WHIRLPOOL SYSTEM

SINK: VITRA FORM GLASS BOWL

TOILET: KOHLER

LIGHTING: OVER SINK: PAOLO PIVA
VANITY: ROBBIA HALF, CASELLA LIGHTING

FITTINGS: INTERNATIONAL FAUCET CO.,
RIVERSTONE

TOWEL BAR: ELEGANTE

TOILET TISSUE HOLDER: ELEGANTE

HOOKS: ELEGANTE

BENCH/STOOL: DA MOTTO STUDIO

ABOVE: *The glass-top vanity has shallow drawers on either side for cosmetic accessories. The light fixtures throughout the room are on dimmers and can be adjusted for putting on makeup, washing up, or relaxing in the whirlpool.*

OPPOSITE: *The sink with its large circular mirror is set into an island in the room, effectively breaking up the bathroom into separate areas. In the foreground is a reflection of the dressing table.*

ABOVE: *With creative reconfiguring on the designer's part, the large glass window adjacent to the tub allows bathers to enjoy marvelous views of the pine, fir, and eucalyptus trees on the grounds.*

LEFT: *The central island of sycamore and cherry wood, with its set-in sink, is designed to accommodate all the necessary storage space for toiletries and towels while dividing the room into four separate areas. The atrium window is in the background.*

OPPOSITE: *The glass-enclosed shower has storage in the built-in bench for easy access to shampoo and soap.*

Monastically Simple

Architect Scott Bromley's New York City home is a clean-lined loft with a view of the Hudson River.

The bathroom evolved out of a total renovation of a space that had once housed an elevator air shaft and a storage room. It is located just off the dressing room, which is, in turn, adjacent to the bedroom. A certain monastic quality is created by its small square footage.

A large gray tile shower area is the centerpiece of this bath and takes up much of its space. Off to one side of the shower is a rectangular bench with a view of midtown Manhattan, which allows Bromley a unique place to sit and read. A curved roll of stainless steel forms the sink; backed by a mirror and flanked by soft gray walls, it adds to the drama of this high-tech bathroom.

ARCHITECT: R. SCOTT BROMLEY

DESIGNER: BROMLEY CALDARI ARCHITECTS

CONTRACTOR: MAXI CONSTRUCTION

FLOOR/WALLS: GLASS TILE

SINK: STAINLESS STEEL, CUSTOM

SHOWER: GLASS TILE

TOILET: KOHLER

LIGHTING: LSI

SHOWER/SINK FITTINGS: KROIN

HOOKS: D-LINE

ABOVE LEFT: *Looking west toward the Hudson River: No blinds or curtains are necessary with this degree of privacy!*

BELOW LEFT: *The open shelves provide storage for bath equipment. A built-in hamper makes sense in this bath and dressing room's layout.*

OPPOSITE: *A traveler's palm tree flourishes in the generous-sized tiled shower*

Farm Fields

Designer Paul Siskin, of the design firm Siskin Valls Inc., collaborated with project architect Claire Weisz of Agrest and Gandelsonas on a new and very contemporary weekend home on the eastern end of Long Island. The multilayered structure is notable for many design features, and particularly for the silo-shaped glass tower that dominates the house. On the ground level the tower houses a circular study; on the second floor, what had originally been intended as a greenhouse was redesigned to expand the size and scope of the master bath.

This marvelously open space affords expansive views of both the potato fields that surround this picturesque resort area and the Atlantic Ocean nearby. The circular theme is maintained throughout the bath, from the circular tub to the two circular sinks and the large globe light hanging from the twenty-foot-high ceiling.

Weisz used the long expanse of the mahogany-fronted double sink to bridge the two distinctly separate areas of this bathroom: the more functional part comprising the shower, bidet, and toilet, and the more luxurious section, with its tub and chaise longue.

Plentiful natural light enables the owners to accessorize the bath with trees and plants, most notably a large Hawaiian ficus plant. At night the bathroom tower—with its dramatic lighting—serves as a beacon to visitors approaching the driveway.

On the floor, comfortably worn kilim rugs in shades of brown, gray, taupe, and peach add color to the pre-

A soft terry-cloth slipcover was used on the chaise, which faces the tub at one end of this circular bathroom. Kilims are scattered throughout the room, warming the marble floor underfoot.

dominantly monochromatic scheme, while softening the steel and marble elements. Siskin notes, "The most important accessory in the bath is the tree. Without it you could feel like you were floating in a fishbowl. It's needed for a sense of scale and to ground you in the space."

ABOVE LEFT: *In keeping with the curved theme, the designer placed a circular tub—complete with massage jets—looking out onto farm fields and toward the Atlantic Ocean.*

CENTER LEFT: *The toilet and bidet are situated behind frosted glass doors. The surrounding walls are white marble.*

BELOW LEFT: *A detail of the white marble tile floor, with woven slippers from Romania.*

OPPOSITE: *On a long wall, the designer made good use of space with these twin sinks by Kohler, which echo the circular shapes of the tower bathroom. Undercounter wooden slats run vertically.*

ARCHITECT: AGREST AND GANDELSONAS/
   DIANA AGREST, PARTNER IN CHARGE/CLAIRE
   WEISZ, PROJECT ARCHITECT
DESIGNER: PAUL SISKIN, SISKIN-VALLS INC.
FLOOR: MARBLE TILE AND WHITE CARRARA
WALLS: GLASS, STAINLESS STEEL, GLUE LAMI-
   NATED RING BEAMS
TUB: AMERICH
SINK: KOHLER
SHOWER: CUSTOM MARBLE TILE
TOILET/BIDET: KOHLER
FITTINGS: CHICAGO FAUCET
TOWEL BAR: CUSTOM

ABOVE: *A view from outside shows the house's multifaceted architectural elements. The bath is on the upper level of the silo-shaped glass tower.*

LEFT: *A pendant is suspended from the ceiling of the tower.*

OPPOSITE: *A wooden hand model sits alongside a catch-all Indonesian box on the ten-foot-long double marble sink.*

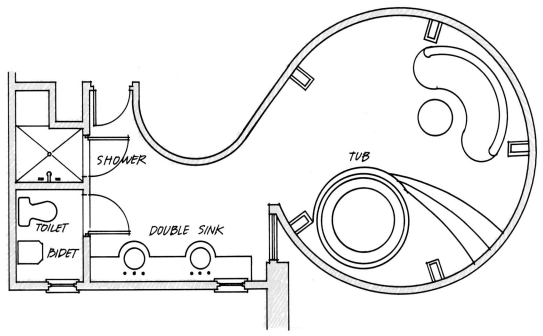

SHOWER

TOILET

BIDET

DOUBLE SINK

TUB

Mahogany & Marble

Working with architect and designer Juan Pablo Molyneux, a New York couple took the unusual route of converting a six-bedroom Park Avenue apartment into a more spacious two-bedroom apartment. One happy side result: a marvelous area in which to construct two large bathrooms, each with its own dressing room and study.

Because the gentleman's bathroom space was literally carved out of the interior of the apartment, adequate lighting was a primary concern of both the owners and the designer. With skillful use of recessed lighting, and in particular the addition of a lighted dome overhead, Molyneux succeeded in creating a lighting scheme that flatters the cool ambience of the marble floor and the old-world elegance of the mahogany paneling.

ABOVE RIGHT: *Bath soaps and crystals housed in elegant jars, designed by Hilton McConnico, are placed on the green marble surround of the tub.*

RIGHT: *For easy access, a hamper and storage space are placed in the mahogany cabinetry flanking the tub.*

OPPOSITE: *The Kohler tub is situated under a mahogany arch in a frame of the same wood. A television set is strategically placed for relaxed viewing.*

ABOVE LEFT: *The elegant entrance to the bath evokes the atmosphere of an exclusive men's club. An expansive lighted dome is overhead.*

ABOVE RIGHT: *The gentleman's dressing room/study stands at one end of the bathroom. The inlaid geometric pattern in the marble floor serves to segment the various elements of this long bathroom.*

LEFT: *The toilet is located in a separate room; its window was finished with tailored Roman shades.*

OPPOSITE: *Skilled use of lighting was crucial in this bathroom, carved out of the interior portion of a New York City apartment building. The window adjacent to the tub utilizes artificial light.*

Approaching from either end of the gentleman's bath, it appears as if one is gazing down a grand hallway. But it is a bath with a twist, comprising a series of rooms, each with its own function. Molyneux notes, "We always thought of this room as an extension of a gentleman's library, so that influenced our choice of materials: the richness of mahogany, the sleekness of marble, and, of course, the sophistication of mirrors."

The green marble floor—of Molyneux's own design—is decorated with inlaid geometric patterns to accentuate the different areas of the bathroom. This technique creates an intimacy and a human dimension in this rather large, architecturally dramatic space.

To further the feeling of intimacy, a long Chippendale-style bench was placed alongside the long wall of the bath opposite the shower area; Regency sconces with pale lemon shades were added on either side. A beveled mirror panel adds élan as well as expansiveness above.

The oversized Molyneux-designed shower features a Scotch shower and a steam bath, both encased in the same green marble used on the floors and walls of the bathroom. Similarly, the large tub is framed by the marble and a hamper is ingeniously built into the cabinet next to it.

One requirement of the owners was abundant storage throughout this room. The magnificent mahogany cabinetry was designed to maximize every inch of space. There is, for example, ample storage in the cabinet adjacent to the bathtub for towels, bathrobes, and other bathroom paraphernalia.

ARCHITECT/DESIGNER: J. P. MOLYNEUX STUDIO LTD.

FLOOR: DESIGNED BY J. P. MOLYNEUX STUDIO LTD.

WALLS: WALL UPHOLSTERY, JULES EDLIN

CEILING AND CROWN MOLDINGS: PAINTED BY WIDENER & ROBINSON

TUB: KOHLER

SINK: KOHLER

SHOWER: J. P. MOLYNEUX STUDIO LTD., CUSTOM

TOILET: KOHLER

LIGHTING: LIGHTOLIER

FITTINGS: HARRINGTON BRASS WORKS, KRAFT

TOWEL BAR: KRAFT

TOILET TISSUE HOLDER: KRAFT

HOOKS: KRAFT

TOWELS/LINENS: PRATESI

SHOWER DOOR: CR SPECIALTIES

And because a Lifecycle with a television set nearby (to catch the early-morning news shows) was one of the owners' first requests, Molyneux built a special exercise niche next to the shower area, complete with a spanking new set of chrome free weights.

LEFT: *A mirrored niche houses the Lifecycle, weights, and exercise area.*

OPPOSITE: *The walls of the spacious shower/ steam bath are lined with the same green marble used throughout the bathroom.*

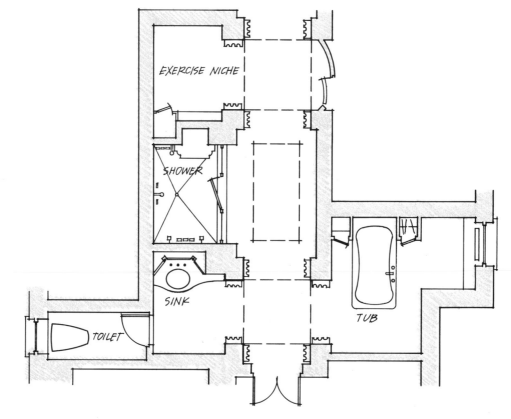

Patinated Modern

Andrea Michaelson opted for a timeless quality in the home in the hills of southern California that she shares with her husband and her two young children. From the outside, the concrete and steel house has a modern look to it. Yet on the inside, careful placement of a few well-chosen pieces against a backdrop of rough gray walls creates a unique charm, a palazzo-like spirit, to the high-ceiling rooms.

Michaelson's bathroom and her husband's are on opposite ends of their master bedroom, and hers leads directly into a well-organized dressing room. The distinct look of her bath was well thought out during the three years she planned the house. As she observes, "The architectural elements are fairly contemporary, so I decided to bring in age and character through the furniture."

ABOVE LEFT: *A deep recess in the wall above the tub contains antique door pulls, turned sideways, upon which to hang towels.*

LEFT: *An essential bathroom ingredient—the scale—rests on the Texan sandstone floor.*

OPPOSITE: *The view from Andrea Michaelson's bath leads toward her dressing room with its silver-leaf doors.*

ABOVE: *The brass basin and fixtures were left unlacquered, resulting in a timeless patina for the custom-designed sink.*

LEFT: *The toilet and bidet, both by Kohler, reinforce the design scheme of this bathroom: clean and unobtrusive. The absence of a door was a deliberate decision on the owner's part.*

OPPOSITE: *The owner discovered the stylish mirrored dressing table prior to the bathroom's renovation and used it for the bath's inspiration. It contrasts well with the horizontal tube lighting.*

The mirrored dressing table was discovered even before she began the design of the bath. She worked its placement into the layout of the room, so that it now holds family photos, perfumes, and hairbrushes, keeping the rest of the counters clear.

The toilet and bidet are in their own three-sided nook—Michaelson wanted them in a separate space, but didn't feel a door was necessary. The sink's floating countertop is higher and deeper than most ("more practical"). Deep recesses in the walls hold towels and bottles, keeping clutter to a minimum, and even the lighting is built into horizontal niches in the walls and mirrors. Sandstone floors from Texas are grouted with cement; the detailed corner tiles were added to counterbalance the plain squares and give the design, in Michaelson's words, "a romantic feel."

ARCHITECT/DESIGNER: ANDREA ELROD MICHAELSON

CONTRACTOR: MARC MICHAELSON

FLOOR: CHARCOAL AND GREEN SLATE

WALLS: CONCRETE

TUB: TILED

SINK: KOHLER

TOILET/BIDET: KOHLER

LIGHTING: TIM THOMAS, ARCHITECTURAL LIGHTING

TOWEL BAR: BOBRICK AND ANTIQUE

TOILET TISSUE HOLDER: BOBRICK

Granite & Steel

Cashmere granite lines the floor and walls of this contemporary powder room in a New York City apartment on Manhattan's Upper East Side. The small bath, designed by Passanella & Klein, Stolzman & Berg, was part of a year-long renovation of the entire apartment. And, as architect Henry Stolzman says, "Our client wanted something surprising, elegant, and unique."

In keeping with these wishes, the lighting was designed to showcase the lines of the room, especially the stone motif, and also to accentuate the backlit mirror.

The random orbital shelf designed by the architects holds a hammered stainless-steel sink; together they work in tandem to form an architectural composition.

ARCHITECT/DESIGNER: PASSANELLA & KLEIN, STOLZMAN & BERG
FLOORS/WALLS: CASHMERE GRANITE
SINK: P. E. GUERIN
TOILET: AMERICAN STANDARD
LIGHTING: JOHNSON SCHWINGHAMMER
SINK FITTINGS: KROIN
WASTEBASKET: CUSTOM

ABOVE RIGHT: *A wooden sculpture from Peru sits atop a custom-designed "waste basket" divided into two sections for paper and linens.*

RIGHT: *The concealed lighting used in this Fifth Avenue powder room was selected more for aesthetics than for illumination. Beneath it, the stainless-steel sink seems to float on its granite backdrop.*

OPPOSITE: *The hammered stainless-steel sink from P. E. Guerin features fixtures made of polished chrome by Kroin.*

Spa

*The seductive and
restorative elements of
the spa experience*

Seaside Spa

Built in 1760, the Connecticut home of design specialist and author Inger McCabe Elliott and her journalist husband, Osborne Elliott, overlooks the active waters of Stonington Harbor.

When the Elliotts commenced their renovation in 1986, they hoped to re-create the strong feeling of light that their New York City apartment, which over-looks the East River, provided them. And in Stonington they had a luxury that few city bathrooms can afford—space!

Their Stonington bathroom easily accommodates a sauna, a tub and shower, a bureau, a dressing room, a linen closet, a washer, and a dryer. The sauna is used reg-ularly on chilly fall and winter weekends, and while the whirlpool is used rarely, the three-spout shower is in daily operation.

Accessible through a secret door off the bedroom and also opening onto the main hallway, the bathroom is, from an aesthetic

RIGHT: *The teak wood bench ensures relaxation in this small sauna.*

OPPOSITE: *The layout of the bath provides for function as well as form, with the sauna and shower at the far end of the room and a whirlpool bath in its center.*

perspective, a reflection of Inger Elliott's eclectic design sensibilities. Mexican glass tiles, which the owner loves for the wonderful light they give off, mix comfortably with stained pine walls and ceilings and the redwood sauna. Antique rag rugs, a nineteenth-century cabinet and mirror, an antique scale, and numerous family pictures in silver frames add to the personal mix of elements that Inger felt essential to this space.

Complementing the lively warmth of the bath's interior is the visual drama of the constantly changing moods and seasons of Stonington Harbor, showcased in this sparkling renovation.

ABOVE LEFT: *A small stackable washer and dryer unit is hidden in a corner of the bath behind a curtain of China Seas fabric designed by Inger Elliott.*

LEFT: *Irregular Mexican glass tiles line the floor and walls of the shower.*

OPPOSITE, ABOVE: *Built-in niches along the sea blue tiled wall hold an assortment of bottles, brushes, and other bath paraphernalia.*

OPPOSITE, BELOW: *A close-up of the tub fixtures and some of the owners' mementos.*

ARCHITECT: NATE MCBRIDE, MCBRIDE & ASSOCIATES

DESIGNER: INGER MCCABE ELLIOTT

CONTRACTOR: PAUL DESCHNES

FLOOR: MEXICAN GLASS TILES

WALLS: MEXICAN GLASS TILES

TUB: KOHLER

SINK: ANTIQUE

SHOWER: MEXICAN GLASS TILE

TOILET: AMERICAN STANDARD

SAUNA: REDWOOD, PAUL DESCHNES

FITTINGS: PAUL ASSOCIATES

HOOKS: ANTIQUE

TOWELS/LINENS: ANTIQUE

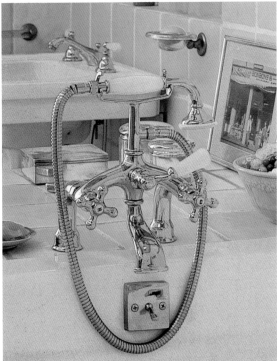

ABOVE: *Creative use of tile means that multitiered built-ins provide unique storage and display spaces.*

LEFT: *A view from the bedroom into the bathroom. A "secret passage" to the bath is created by the door, which holds bookshelves.*

OPPOSITE: *Just a few steps off the bath, French doors open out to the deck and Long Island Sound beyond.*

Reservoir Refuge

Kitty Hawks and Larry Lederman's home in Westchester County, New York, overlooks a serene nine-acre reservoir. Taking their lead from the exquisite setting and working with "1100"—a New York–based architectural firm—Hawks, who is a leading New York interior designer, and Lederman redesigned the house to reflect the relationship of this property to the land and water views surrounding it.

The bath itself is located just off the owners' bedroom on the lower level, and has a door opening onto an outside space complete with a shower and a hot tub. Not only does the bath offer immediate access to the outdoors, but its interior is also very much influenced by the dramatic natural landscape beyond. The decorative elements that Hawks added, such as a grouping of nineteenth-century alphabet engravings, a

ABOVE RIGHT: *A close-up of the often-used outdoor shower. Scrub brush and towel await the next bather.*

RIGHT: *The moss-covered stone bench.*

OPPOSITE: *Designer Kitty Hawks's bathroom opens onto this path, surrounded by holly, ferns, and rhododendrons, which leads to the hot tub. The outdoor shower is next to the door.*

nineteenth-century Indonesian sunburst, a pair of brass candlesticks, and two Chinese rugs, serve to heighten the natural clarity of the bluestone elements found in the tiles, bath, and vanity slabs.

Changes were mainly cosmetic. Hawks explains, "We knew what we wanted to do from the start." Towels and linens are kept in cabinets above the hamper opposite the toilet, which is in a separate room at the end of the bathroom. Everything else is stored in the vanity drawers.

The owners view their bath as a place of repose and refuge, and the components of this space are both contemporary and sensual. Hawks says, "The bathroom has always been an important place for me. I react strongly to these rooms, perhaps because of the state of vulnerability they invoke, so a comfortable space is most important, no matter what the scale."

Stone steps and slabs outside lead to the hot tub nestled in the hillside among holly, rhododendron, ferns, patches of pachysandra, and ivy. Two Japanese candle lanterns flank the stone seat next to the tub, making this corner a most private space that is, nonetheless, open to the outdoors.

Opposite the tub sits a moss-covered stone bench, which becomes a natural shelf for the outdoor shower with its oversized showerhead and simple faucets. A wire fruit treillage holds towels and soaps. And in keeping with the relationship between this property and the surrounding waters, gently worn slate steps lead down from the hot tub and shower through the forest to the reservoir below.

ABOVE LEFT: *The glass-walled shower is next to the tub. A slate slab bench was added for sitting or holding shower paraphernalia.*

ABOVE RIGHT: *A view toward the door leading to the outside shower. An old hat rack holds an assortment of sun hats.*

OPPOSITE, ABOVE: *Nineteenth-century alphabet engravings line the wall above the tub. Recessed high-hat lighting emanates from the ceiling.*

OPPOSITE, BELOW: *A nineteenth-century Indonesian sunburst hangs in the enclosed toilet. Local slate covers the sink counter.*

ARCHITECTS: DAVID PISCUSKAS, JUERGEN RHEIM, 1100 ARCHITECT

DESIGNER: KITTY HAWKS

FLOOR: LOCAL SLATE AND BLUESTONE

WALLS: DECORATIVE PAINTING, CHUCK HETTINGER

OUTDOOR HOT TUB: CALDERA CASCADE

TUB: SUNRISE SPECIALTY

SINK: AMERICAN STANDARD

SHOWER FITTINGS: SPEAKMAN

SHOWER DOOR: 1100 ARCHITECT, CUSTOM

TOILET: AMERICAN STANDARD

TUB FITTINGS: WATERWORKS

SINK FITTINGS: SPEAKMAN

TOWELS/LINENS: MARTEX

Eastern Delights

The architectural design team of Jed Johnson and Alan Wanzenberg was commissioned by the owner of Twin Farms, a country inn complex located just outside of Woodstock, Vermont, to re-create the feel of a traditional Japanese *furo*, or communal bath, within the clean architectural space of a Vermont barn structure.

In keeping with the Zen-like serenity of this quiet space, accessorization is minimal: a simple wooden folding chair, a container for soaps, brushes, and towels, and an understated overhead copper light fixture designed by Louis Poulsen. The sliding shoji screens complement the mosaic-lined rectangular tub, where the temperature is kept at 104 degrees. Adjacent to the tub is a postbath shower, which has plaster walls and a terracotta–colored concrete floor along with an old-fashioned chain pull that releases only cold water.

ABOVE RIGHT: *Looking into the tub with its blue mosaic walls and underwater bench. A supply of towels is kept within arm's reach.*

OPPOSITE: *The temperature in this Vermont Japanese furo is kept at a constant 104 degrees. The accent is on simplicity, with such elements as the unadorned copper light fixture overhead.*

ARCHITECT: ALAN WANZENBERG, SCOTT CORNELIUS, DESIGNER; ALAN WANZENBERG ARCHITECTS, P.C.

DESIGNER: JED JOHNSON, VANCE BURKE, ASSOCIATE; JED JOHNSON & ASSOC., INC.

FLOOR: COLORED CONCRETE

WALLS: PLASTER

TUB: CERAMIC TILE

SINK: AMERICAN STANDARD OVALIN UNDERCOUNTER

TOILET: AMERICAN STANDARD LEXINGTON

LIGHTING: COPPER OVERHEAD FIXTURES DESIGNED BY LOUISE POULSEN

SHOWER FITTINGS: SPEAKMAN

SINK FITTINGS: CHICAGO FAUCET

A Private Spa

Designed by Glenn Gissler, the steam room/bath in Caroline Hirsch's Long Island home is adjacent to a state-of-the-art home gymnasium. A glass door opens onto the eight-foot-by-eight-foot tiled steam room, with a built-in bench to seat comfortably up to six people after a workout. Additional body sprays supplement the oversized showerhead.

The creamy taupe bathroom walls provide a muted backdrop for the large black soapstone sink. One long towel bar—more than six feet of polished nickel—holds a multitude of towels for the steam bath occupants. The design of the gym itself was influenced by the early-twentieth-century exercise rooms of some of the great American spas.

ABOVE RIGHT: *The 8-by-8-foot steam bath has a marble seat extending along two walls.*

BELOW RIGHT: *The streamlined towel bar—in excess of 6 feet—affords plenty of space for steam-room towels.*

OPPOSITE: *Looking toward the steam room and bathroom from the well-equipped exercise room. Old wooden weights contrast with the state-of-the-art treadmill that towers over them.*

ARCHITECT: FRANCIS FLEETWOOD

DESIGNER: GLENN GISSLER DESIGN, INC.

FLOOR/BASEBOARD: AMERICAN OLEAN

COUNTER: OILED SOAPSTONE

SINK: KOHLER

SHOWER TILES: AMERICAN OLEAN

SHOWER DOOR: DISTINCTIVE SHOWER DOORS

TOILET: ST. THOMAS CREATIONS

STEAMROOM: MR. STEAM

FITTINGS: HARRINGTON BRASS WORKS

TOWEL BAR: URBAN ARCHAEOLOGY

TISSUE HOLDER: URBAN ARCHAEOLOGY

Ten Thousand Waves

Nestled in the foothills of the Sangre de Cristo Mountains, in the outskirts of Santa Fe, is Ten Thousand Waves. This Japanese-style spa offers an invigorating choice of hot tubs, cold plunges, saunas, herbal wraps, salt glows, and massages to the many visitors who flock there each year.

Founder and owner Duke Klauck, a student of Japanese culture for many years, patterned Ten Thousand Waves after hot-spring resorts in the mountains of Japan. The traditional *furo*, or communal hot tub, communal cold plunges and saunas are therefore available, as well as individual tubs. The mingling of southwestern and Japanese design influences provides a peaceful ambience.

With its own changing room, shower, tub, sauna, and cooling berth, the "Imperial Ofuro" represents the ultimate in luxurious bathing. The room is open on one side, with a private balcony looking toward the mountains. The soothing colors of sea and sky are reflected in the tiled floor and the mosaic tub.

Adjacent to the sauna is the cooling berth for post–hot tub and sauna relaxation. With its walls of Aspen pine and its Philippine mahogany bench, the cooling berth becomes a room unto itself, covered by a sloping cedar shingled roof. An overarching glass ceiling provides natural light in the day and views of the star-filled Santa Fe sky in the evening.

Santa Fe's Ten Thousand Waves offers visitors a wide choice of bath and spa choices, from hot tubs to herbal wraps. The Watsu tub, or waterfall tub, is nestled in a secluded area for underwater massages.

cold plunge

DESIGNER: TEN THOUSAND WAVES STAFF

TUB: WOODEN, FRANCISCAN WOODWORKS

COLD PLUNGE: FRANCISCAN WOODWORKS

SINK: HAND-THROWN POTTERY

ABOVE: *A colorful array of stacked towels inside the dressing room.*

OPPOSITE, ABOVE: *A glass sloped ceiling provides abundant New Mexican sunlight to the Imperial Ofuro. This view looks toward the entrance, with the cooling berth on the left.*

OPPOSITE, BELOW LEFT: *The cold plunge—temperatures usually range in the low 50s—is constructed from Australian Jarrah wood.*

OPPOSITE, BELOW RIGHT: *Looking toward the Sangre de Cristo mountains from the Imperial Ofuro.*

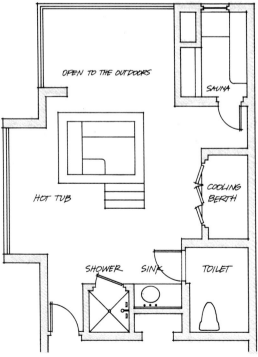

OPEN TO THE OUTDOORS

SAUNA

HOT TUB

COOLING BERTH

SHOWER   SINK   TOILET

Idiosyncratic

*Baths that venture
beyond the traditional
vernacular*

Art Deco Delight

Many people consider the bathroom a place of refuge in their home. Not Phyllis Paulson, the owner of this brilliantly colored bathroom in a 1929 apartment building in the Pacific Heights section of San Francisco. She once hosted a cocktail party in this room using colorful fruit sponges for name tags!

Designer Robert Federighi, working with Paulson, was inspired by the art deco feeling of the apartment in his design approach to the bathroom. The existing green tile wall, with black trim, and the marble floor were left untouched. Stainless-steel pyramid caps were placed above the sink to camouflage the old black tile soap and cup holders.

The centerpiece of the room—a sizable clear glass bowl sink with stylized dolphin faucets and stainless-steel legs—was added, along with a new shower featuring recessed lighting and etched initials in its glass doors. Pleated stainless-steel trim in the shower matches the stainless-and-glass cabinet. Mirrored on the back, this cabinet has abundant space; Federighi included electrical outlets in the bottom drawer for Paulson's hair dryer and electric toothbrush. Within the shower stall itself is a tiny marble cabinet that houses shampoos and soaps, keeping them out of view when not needed.

The custom-designed dolphin-shaped faucets and the oversized glass bowl sink were both created by the bathroom's designer, Robert Federighi.

DESIGNER: ROBERT FEDERIGHI

FLOOR: CARRARA MARBLE

WALLS: ORIGINAL 1930'S TILES

TUB: AMERICAN STANDARD

SINK: ROBERT FEDERIGHI, SPECIALTY GLASS &
MARBLE

SHOWER: ROBERT FEDERIGHI, CUSTOM

TOILET: AMERICAN STANDARD

LIGHTING: HALO

SHOWER FITTINGS: DORNBRACHT

TUB FITTINGS: AMERICAN STANDARD

SINK FITTINGS: ROBERT FEDERIGHI, CUSTOM

HEATED TOWEL BAR: RUNTAL

HOOKS: DORNBRACHT

TOWELS/LINENS: ALAN LADD

SHOWER CURTAIN: ETCHINGS

WASTEBASKET: BED AND BATH

STAINLESS-STEEL WORK: ANDRUS SHEET METAL

ABOVE LEFT: *The glass and pleated stainless-steel cabinet next to the shower is mirrored on all three walls, creating a visual treat.*

LEFT: *A close-up of the dolphin-style faucet.*

OPPOSITE: *In the renovation, the owner retained the existing black-trimmed green tile and the marble floor. Both features suggest the art deco theme of other rooms in the apartment.*

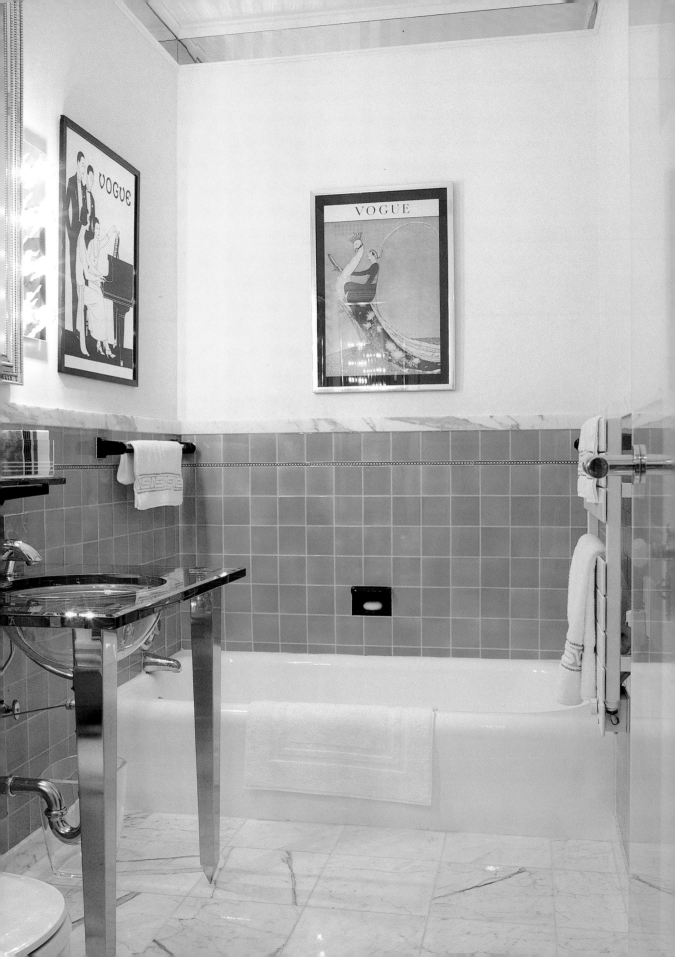

Vermont
Vernacular

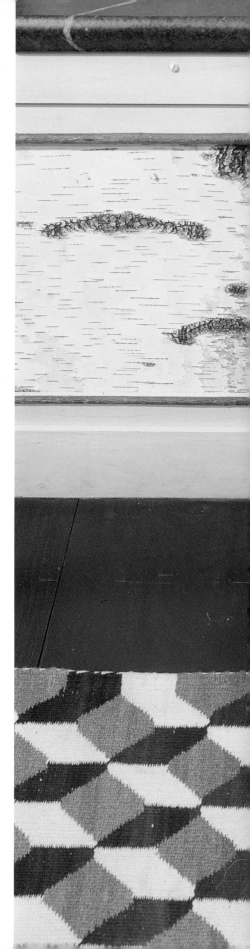

Take three separate guest cottages at an inn located in a most idyllic setting in southern Vermont, add the talented architectural design groups of Jed Johnson and Alan Wanzenberg, and the result is three very special bath and dressing rooms (along with equally individual bed and sitting rooms).

As Wanzenberg observed, "Because the clientele of Twin Farms is made up of well-seasoned and sophisticated travelers, we wanted this New England setting to have not only luxurious accommodations, but ones that would be unique. Each cottage evokes different memories in people, and that was important to us—this strong aesthetic of memory. We wanted something quirky, and a bit different."

The team began with an overall design concept, and then followed up with the plan for each room. Inspired by a spectrum of design sources, from traditional Vermont barns and farmhouses to Russian, Japanese, and Adirondack architecture to the Colonial Revival designs of the 1930s, Johnson and Wanzenberg came up with three individual cottages: the Treehouse, the Perch, and the Studio.

RIGHT: *A detail of the Treehouse's tub surround and carpet.*

OPPOSITE: *A long green hall leads to the bathroom in the Perch. A whimsical underwater scene of tropical fish and multicolored coral, hand-painted by Boyd-Reath Studios of New York City, runs above the green paneled walls.*

ARCHITECT: ALAN WANZENBERG, SCOTT CORNELIUS, DESIGNER; ALAN WANZENBERG ARCHITECTS, P.C.

DESIGNER: JED JOHNSON, VANCE BURKE, ASSOCIATE; JED JOHNSON & ASSOC., INC.

FLOOR: EBONIZED PINE

WALLS: WHITE CEDAR PANELING, RED PLASTER

TUB: KOHLER

SINK: CUSTOM

SHOWER: SPLIT FACE STONE

TOILET: AMERICAN STANDARD

BIDET: AMERICAN STANDARD

LIGHTING: CUSTOM

FITTINGS: BARWIL TRADITIONAL TAPS

TOWEL BAR: CUSTOM

TOILET TISSUE HOLDER: URBAN ARCHAEOLOGY

HOOKS: URBAN ARCHAEOLOGY

The Treehouse

In the Treehouse, the designers wanted to work in the rustic Adirondack style, but with a Brighton Pavilion twist. An eight-foot-tall armoire made of birch, with "twig" metal pulls, leads into the dressing area of the bath. Richly colored cinnabar walls and accessories bring the extra-wide wainscoting alive. The long expanse of a double sink is topped with handsome black marble and provides needed counter space. The large tub is encased in a birch-bark surround. Color choices for the Treehouse were directed by a dramatic geometric custom-made wool rug that lies in the center of the marble floor. Explains Wanzenberg, "We typically work up color schemes from the carpets as if they're dominant art pieces."

ABOVE RIGHT: *A banquette with a fabric-covered cushion is adjacent to the shower.*

RIGHT: *The double sink has brushed stainless-steel legs and towel racks. A pair of matching Adirondack-style mirrors hangs above.*

OPPOSITE, ABOVE: *This bathroom evokes the feeling of a treehouse right down to the birch-bark tub surround. A paneled wall separates the bathing area from the dressing area.*

OPPOSITE, BELOW: *A close-up of the birch armoire reveals the twig pulls on the doors and drawers.*

The Perch

Fish motifs and a sense of humor dictated the design of the Perch. Here, the dressing room and the water closet are dramatized by the multicolored fish motif painted by Jim Boyd, from Boyd-Reath Studios of New York, on the upper walls of the hallway. The main part of the bathroom has a more masculine feel. Such deft touches as a wooden "cock fighting" chair in the corner, old-fashioned cream tiles on the walls, and a glass-fronted armoire add to this ambience.

ARCHITECT: ALAN WANZENBERG, SCOTT CORNELIUS, DESIGNER; ALAN WANZENBERG ARCHITECTS, P.C.

DESIGNER: JED JOHNSON, VANCE BURKE, ASSOCIATE; JED JOHNSON & ASSOC., INC.

FLOOR: TEAK

WALLS: CERAMIC TILE

FISH MOTIF PAINTING: JIM BOYD, BOYD-REATH STUDIOS

TUB: CUSTOM, COPPER

SINK: AMERICAN STANDARD

SHOWER: CERAMIC TILE

TOILET: AMERICAN STANDARD

BIDET: AMERICAN STANDARD

FITTINGS: BARWIL TRADITIONAL TAPS

TOWEL BAR: URBAN ARCHAEOLOGY

TOILET TISSUE HOLDER: URBAN ARCHAEOLOGY

HOOKS: URBAN ARCHAEOLOGY

TOP: *A tin fish bought in a Paris flea market adds a whimsical touch.*

ABOVE: *An antique wooden box, for bath paraphernalia, sits on the tub's marble surround.*

ABOVE RIGHT: *The five-sided tub is lined with copper. Sheer muslin curtains frame the windows.*

RIGHT: *The shaving mirror extends over the marble sink with its antique wooden fish decoy. The backsplash continues the fish motif.*

OPPOSITE, ABOVE: *The Perch's sink area is built into a niche.*

OPPOSITE, BELOW: *The shower area maintains the look of a men's club, with brick-shaped tiles and dark wood framing the door. To the left, a beveled-glass-fronted armoire stores towels.*

The Studio

The Studio was translated from a wish, on the designers' part, to create "a space that an artist would feel comfortable working in, as well as being comfortable for a guest." Veined white marble sheaths three fourths of the bathroom walls, framed by sturdy-looking maple molding that also surrounds the mirrors, windows, and closets. Again, a geometric-patterned rug was a starting point for the room's palette. Three flash heaters are required to fill the huge canted corner tub (also featured in the Perch bathroom) that is, without doubt, the jewel in this well-appointed space.

ABOVE LEFT: *Towels hang on a circular towel ring made of nickel. A utilitarian shaving mirror is to the right.*

LEFT: *The floor is Mexican terra-cotta with a black marble border running around the room. The rug adds a black, white, beige, and cinnabar design.*

OPPOSITE: *The Studio bath features a spacious tub and white marble walls. A pair of framed windows, with matching framed mirrors, allows generous light and air into this space.*

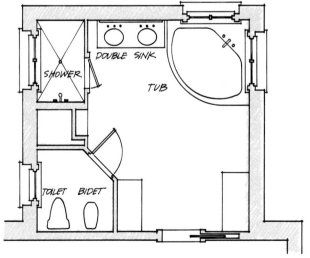

ARCHITECT: ALAN WANZENBERG, SCOTT
CORNELIUS, DESIGNER; ALAN
WANZENBERG ARCHITECTS, P.C.

DESIGNER: JED JOHNSON, VANCE BURKE,
ASSOCIATE; JED JOHNSON & ASSOC., INC.

FLOOR: H&R JOHNSON TILE AND MARBLE

WALLS: MARBLE

TUB: CUSTOM, COPPER

SINK: CUSTOM

SHOWER: MARBLE

TOILET: AMERICAN STANDARD

BIDET: AMERICAN STANDARD

FITTINGS: BARWIL TRADITIONAL TAPS

TOWEL BAR: URBAN ARCHAEOLOGY

TOILET TISSUE HOLDER: URBAN
ARCHAEOLOGY

HOOKS: URBAN ARCHAEOLOGY

SHOWER

DOUBLE SINK

TUB

TOILET   BIDET

A Reading Room

The guest room of this Long Island weekend house was, before substantial renovation, the master bedroom and bathroom of the original house. After a new wing with three bedrooms and three baths was added, this section became a guest room with a bath and dressing room and, quite literally, a library.

The inspiration for this space was, according to its designer, derived from an "Anglo-Indian theme," creating a room that would blend easily into the English country feel of the rest of the house. Designer Stephanie Stokes, who had earlier completed the owners' New York City apartment, also knew that these two avid readers required additional space for their overflow of books—hence the idea to turn the room into a library. It actually does triple duty: as a dressing room/bath for out-of-town guests; as the "office loo" for those using the media room next door; and, of course, as a quiet retreat in which to get away and read. The green-paneled library dominates the space, and the shower, sink, and toilet are hidden in bays behind the two large bookcases.

As in any reading area, correct lighting is paramount. Natural light comes in from the east and south windows and through a skylight over the shower and basin area.

Stokes had the bookcases' woodwork painted dark green, chosen to complement the Edwardian green wallpaper from Clarence House that the owners fell in love with at first sight. Its pattern reinforces the geometric layout of the room. A folding deck chair with a small reading lamp nearby completes this corner of quietude.

Antique brass fittings have been added to the Empress Green marble counter with its set-in white porcelain sink.

ARCHITECT: STEPHANIE STOKES, INC.

DESIGNER: STEPHANIE STOKES

ARCHITECTURAL, INTERIOR, AND CABINETRY
  DESIGN: BENJAMIN HUNTINGTON

FLOOR: SISAL; PATTERSON, FLYNN, AND
  MARTIN. KIRKSTONE FROM SOUTHAMPTON
  GALLERY OF MARBLE AND TILE

WALLS: EDWARDIAN MEDALLION WALLPAPER,
  CLARENCE HOUSE

SINK: KOHLER

SHOWER: ARCHITECTURAL DETAILS, CUSTOM
  SHOWER BODY

TOILET: ARCHITECTURAL DETAILS

LIGHTING: HOWARD KAPLAN'S BATH SHOP

SHOWER FITTINGS: ARCHITECTURAL DETAILS

SINK FITTINGS: HOWARD KAPLAN'S BATH SHOP

TOWEL BAR: HOWARD KAPLAN'S BATH SHOP

TOILET TISSUE HOLDER: HOWARD KAPLAN'S
  BATH SHOP

HOOKS: HOWARD KAPLAN'S BATH SHOP

TOWELS/LINENS: JOHN MATOUK & CO.

ABOVE LEFT: *A Staffordshire dog, from the owners' collection of porcelain dogs and horses, accessorizes the book-lined built-in cabinets.*

OPPOSITE: *A rattan and wood deck chair, with a mustard-colored throw, is perfect for after-bath luxuriating. The caramel sisal carpet and the antique brass duck towel holder add to the luxe setting.*

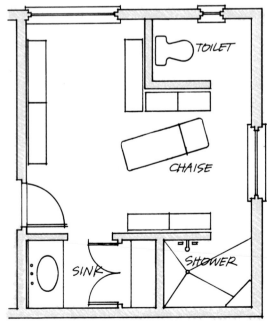

A Pugilistic Character

The attic of a Pennsylvania farmhouse was converted by designer Jeffrey Bilhuber into a bath and steam room with a spacious exercise room. With track lighting overhead and a Bilhuber-designed wool carpet on the floor, the state-of-the-art exercise equipment mingles nicely with a collection of iconoclastic accessories, chosen by the owners and the designer. It is, in Bilhuber's words, "eighteenth-century modern."

Bold strokes, strong architecture, clean lines—the design of these rooms emanates strength. Nineteenth-century wooden gears that Bilhuber placed along one wall symbolize power and energy, and one of them actually functions as a spout, pouring water into the sink below. Drums from Taos, New Mexico, serve as evocative occasional tables.

Rough-cut pine planks, which run horizontally around the exercise room and its slanted ceilings, reinforce the feeling of vigor. A nineteenth-century baptismal font from Guatemala has been transformed into a rugged basin, balancing the visual weight of the gears above; its wooden cabinet opens for towel storage.

Nineteenth-century boxing prints line the walls of the exercise room. In the bath, a simple white pedestal sink is flanked by more pugilistic prints and complemented by the straightforward lines of a wood-framed American mirror.

Antique wooden gears and drum tables from Taos, New Mexico, add a dimension of warmth to the decidedly state-of-the-art exercise machines.

ABOVE LEFT: *A steady stream of water from the metal spout of the oversized gear flows into a 19th-century baptismal font of Guatemalan origin.*

ABOVE RIGHT: *An American wood-framed mirror hangs above the simple pedestal sink with slim-lined lights on either side, while a bronze rooster, crafted in France, sits underneath.*

OPPOSITE, ABOVE LEFT: *The rough cut of the pine-planked walls and floor reinforces the sophisticated "country" ambience of this Pennsylvania farmhouse's bathroom.*

DESIGNER:	JEFFREY BILHUBER, BILHUBER, INC.
FLOOR:	BLEACHED PINE; WOOL MOROCCAN RUG DESIGNED BY BILHUBER
WALLS:	ROUGH-HEWN PINE PLANK
MIRROR:	ANTIQUE
BASIN:	GUATEMALAN BAPTISMAL FONT
SHOWER:	KOHLER
TOILET:	KOHLER
FITTINGS:	KRAFT
TOWEL BAR:	KRAFT

OPPOSITE, ABOVE RIGHT: *An assemblage of antique wooden gears hangs over the basin, which sits on a vertically planked cabinet; underneath is abundant towel storage.*

OPPOSITE, BELOW: *Framed 19th- and 20th-century boxing prints line the horizontal pine-planked walls of this bathroom/exercise room created by Jeffrey Bilhuber. Geometric-patterned wool carpeting anchors the space.*

The Men's Room

A visitor to Charles Morris Mount and Harold Gordon's weekend home in eastern Long Island will, undoubtedly, vividly recall one feature of the bathroom, namely, its full-sized restaurant-style urinal.

Mount, a well-known restaurant designer, selected granite for much of the wall and floor space. The focal point of the bathroom is a translucent wall of carved glass blocks. These same glass walls flank two sides of the shower, where Grohe shower fixtures seem to float on the surface of the granite wall.

The space that contains the sink is also granite-lined. A Franke stainless-steel bowl cuts into its center, while two Formica cabinets on either end hold bathroom paraphernalia.

The urinal itself was chosen for its convenience and also to rebel, in Mount's words, "against seat lifting."

ABOVE RIGHT: *An unusual yet practical touch: the commercial-style urinal from Kohler.*

OPPOSITE: *Two walls of translucent glass blocks are juxtaposed with the solid granite wall of the shower.*

DESIGNER: CHARLES MORRIS MOUNT

CONTRACTOR: BOB BAYLEY, CAMP CEDER DESIGN

CABINET FABRICATOR: D. REIS

FLOOR/WALLS/COUNTERTOPS: GRANITE TILE; DESIGN SUPPLY, STONE SOURCE

WALLS: BENJAMIN MOORE, LINEN WHITE

GLASS BLOCKS: PITTSBURG CORNING

SINK: FRANKE

SHOWER: GROHE

TOILET: KOHLER

URINAL: KOHLER

LAMINATE: FORMICA

WALL SCONCE: BEGA LIGHTING

HIGH HATS: LIGHTOLIER

SHOWER FITTINGS: GROHE

SINK FITTINGS: KROIN

TOILET TISSUE HOLDER: KROIN

MIRROR: GULLANS INTERNATIONAL

Mountain Views

Jay and Elizabeth Smith were frequent visitors to Santa Fe over the years, and when they decided to build their home there, their goal was to create a design that would capture the distinctive local look they had come to admire during their many visits. Of equal importance to them was that their house take advantage of the breathtaking views that their land offered. The dramatic site presents views in every direction, from the Jemez Mountains in the west to the Sangre de Cristo Mountains in the east. Tesuque and Espanola are to the north, as is, on the clearest of days, Colorado.

Santa Fe—based architect Christopher Purvis made full use of these views when he worked with the Smiths to achieve the desired effect in their year-long construction. Their bath, in particular, was designed with these incredible vistas in mind. As Elizabeth Smith notes, "The room itself is just off the master bedroom. We hoped to create a bath that would reflect the image of the outdoors. The results were perfect." A window was even installed in the shower strictly for the views. Mud walls and Chinese slate were chosen to blend with the natural tones of the earth. Wooden religious artifacts, indigenous to the Southwest, complete the accessorization of this room.

The overall aesthetic is one of soft lines and colors that complement the pure light so characteristic of this part of the world.

Windows over the slate and porcelain tub open onto the Sangre de Cristo Mountains, while a kiva fireplace produces natural warmth for the bather. Softly curved walls and slate flooring reinforce the Southwestern appeal.

ARCHITECT:	CHRISTOPHER PURVIS, ARCHITECTS SANTA FE
CONTRACTOR:	CHRIS CLEMENS, CLEMENS CONSTRUCTION
WALLS:	CUSTOM MIX AND PLASTER
TUBS:	AQUS
SINK:	KOHLER
SHOWER:	ELECTRONIC ULTRA-VALVE CONTROL SYSTEM
TOILET:	KOHLER
LIGHTING:	HALO
SINK FITTINGS:	CHICAGO FAUCET
TOWEL BAR:	CUSTOM

ABOVE LEFT: *Southwestern details add drama to the sink.*

ABOVE: *Windows and skylight in the slate-walled shower open to the magnificent landscape and sky.*

LEFT: *The beginning of a perfect soak: candle, bath oil, and rolled towels.*

OPPOSITE: *A small child's chair sits beneath a painting of the Virgin Mary. A built-in niche holds firewood for the kiva and, right, a medicine cabinet is disguised behind a hand-carved door.*

Children's Hour

Muralist Leslie Horan Simon and architect Paul Krause collaborated on this child's bathroom in an apartment on New York's Central Park West. The cherry wood used in the room, which was originally the master bath, reflects the abundant use of this wood throughout the spacious apartment. Architect Krause added a plaster vaulted ceiling to take advantage of the room's generous height. Halfway up the wall there are two different sizes of a tile that Simon painted lime green since the original gray was "no fun for a kid's bath."

Simon took eight working days to create the mural, which, she says, "came directly from my imagination. I think I have a real sensitivity toward children's rooms." A landscape painter for many years, Simon often looks to nature for inspiration in her work and, in this project, she chose a "wetlands" theme and added a collection of *Sesame Street* characters to make it, in her words, "friendly, happy, and bright, as well as peaceful and serene."

Prior to beginning the mural, Simon had all the wood refinished and selected colors to match those used in the adjoining bedroom. She first painted the large trees, the water, and the horizon lines, adding Big Bird, Bert, Ernie, and the vegetation later. The final detail was the "wiggly, waterlike" paint on the outside of the tub.

The ultimate judge of the project—an energetic two-year-old—has given a resounding vote of approval (an enthusiastic Wow!) and beams with delight at the mural that lights up this bath.

A rubber duckie and a large teddy bear protectively flank the young occupant of this child's bathroom in a New York City apartment.

ARCHITECT: PAUL KRAUSE

DESIGNER: LESLIE HORAN SIMON

FLOOR: PATTERSON, FLYNN, MARTIN, MANGES, INC.

WALLS: AMERICAN OLEAN TILE

TUB: URBAN ARCHAEOLOGY

SINK: KOHLER

TOILET: KOHLER

LIGHTING: URBAN ARCHAEOLOGY

FITTINGS: CHICAGO

TOWEL BAR: URBAN ARCHAEOLOGY

HOOKS: URBAN ARCHAEOLOGY

TOWELS/LINENS: RALPH LAUREN HOME COLLECTION

LEFT: *A couple of friendly characters peek out of the large hand-painted mural that dominates the bathroom.*

BELOW LEFT: *The brass and porcelain fittings lend old-fashioned elegance to the generous-sized tub.*

OPPOSITE, ABOVE LEFT: *The tiled shower was built into a corner of this small bath; a frosted outer door provides privacy.*

OPPOSITE, ABOVE RIGHT: *The large frosted glass window above the tub provides both light and privacy. The half-wall separates the small room into two areas.*

OPPOSITE, BELOW: *A white Corian counter surrounds the sink, with ample room for storage in the drawers and cabinets.*

Mood Indigo

The colors of South Florida and the owner's love of the Southwest were the inspiration for this contemporary bath in a home owned by Carol Meredith and located between the Atlantic Ocean and the Intercoastal Waterway, not far from Miami.

Working with his associate, Nelson de Leon, architect Max Wolfe Sturman joined together the bedroom and bath by means of a thick, arched opening. Sturman was able to create the vibrantly textured blue backdrop for the bath by utilizing pure pigments, which were premixed into the plaster; he experimented with various trowel techniques and then sprayed color mixes onto the almost-cured surfaces.

As to the accessories, Sturman notes, "We used a minimalist approach, selecting a few antique sculptures, *tarahumara* (pottery pieces), and *retablos* (tin art pieces)."

ARCHITECT/DESIGNER: MAX WOLFE STURMAN, ARCHITECTS, INC.

FLOORS: ENDURANCE FLOOR CO., HEART PINE FLOORS

WALLS: INTEGRALLY COLORED PLASTER

TUB: VERMONT GREENSTONE, CHS, INC.

SINK: PHYLRICH

SHOWER: MARCITE, VERMONT GREENSTONE

TOILET & BIDET: KOHLER

WHIRLPOOL: CHS, INC.

LIGHTING: LIGHTOLIER; ALCO

FITTINGS: PHYLRICH, BRASS

TOWEL BAR: BRASS, CUSTOM

LINENS: GARNET HILL

ABOVE RIGHT: *The shower area, with its antique copper showerhead and four body sprays, contains a large built-in stone bench.*

RIGHT: *The Vermont stone custom-furnished tub, built on-site, has six whirlpool jets.*

OPPOSITE: *Antique tin art pieces rest on the table in the dressing area.*

Romantic

*The bath as
retreat and refuge*

Theatrical Memories

Designer, restaurateur (The Ivy, Ivy at The Shore), and owner of the chic furnishings shop, Indigo Seas, Lynn von Kersting and her equally talented husband and partner, Richard Irving (L.A. Desserts), immediately fell in love with the Hollywood Hills home of film director George Cukor when it came on the market.

With a baby on the way—India, now seven—the couple realized that the one element missing in this enchanting home was a master bedroom and bathroom suite. Tearing down what had been a small guest room and a series of crumbling concrete changing rooms, they created a pair of luxuriously appointed dressing/bathrooms that mesh with the rest of the house.

An oversized custom-made tub, with a beaded ceramic tile surface, dominates von Kersting's cream-toned bathroom. The tub surround of banker's green marble allows ample space for her very personal collection of framed letters and inscribed portraits of Colette, Sarah Bernhardt, and Eleanora Duse, among others, along with an assortment of blue and white nineteenth-century Moroccan jars, and one of her favorite touches, old-fashioned roses. Above the surround, on glass shelves, are piled new Porthault linens, "mixed in," she says, "with old Porthault linens from my Aunt Holly's apartment in Paris."

The deep green marble surround of the tub is the stage for an assortment of the owner's cherished collection of old photographs, letters, and memorabilia. The mirrored squares add another dimension to this corner.

Lining the walls are a series of Léon Bakst watercolor designs for the Ballets Russes. Above the green marble vanity, a collection of Venetian theatrical crowns, as well as her own theatrical crowns from various productions (*Lady Macbeth, Gertrudis the Queen, Cleopatra*), hangs on the elaborate gilt mirror.

And, courtesy of a hidden sound system, musical recordings of early Caruso and swing music from the 1920s and '30s waft through these rooms as a poignant reminder of the Cukor days.

ABOVE LEFT: *The ornate gilt mirror holds theatrical crowns—some Venetian and some from Lynn von Kersting's days with the Lee Strasberg Studio. Generous shelving for bath towels is reflected in the mirror.*

LEFT: *A view into the length of the bathroom, with the large tub set in between columns. At the end of the room is concealed shelving. The well-worn white rectangular tile on the floor suggests a patina of age.*

OPPOSITE: *The oversized tub has a beaded ceramic tile surface. Overhead lights are on dimmers for control and towels are within easy reach, while the mirrored walls double the size of the space.*

DESIGNER: LYNN VON KERSTING FOR INDIGO SEAS
FLOOR: WHITE BLOCK MARBLE
TUB: CUSTOM BEADED CERAMIC TILE; GREEN MARBLE
SINK: GREEN MARBLE
TOWELS/LINENS: PORTHAULT LINENS

The Gold Bathroom

The Evergreen House in Baltimore—formerly the home of Ambassador T. Harrison Garrett and his wife, the art patron Alice Whitridge—is considered one of the grandest in Maryland and is on the National Register of Historic Places. The forty-eight-room, three-story Classical Revival mansion, now owned by Johns Hopkins University, has a rich architectural heritage. One of its most magnificent rooms is the gold bathroom. Renovated in the 1880s, it featured impressive technology for its time: hot and cold running water and steam heat. The builder, Charles L. Carson, working with the firm of Herter Brothers, installed unpolished marble mosaic floor and walls in shades of

ABOVE LEFT: *The stained-glass window is attributed to Tiffany Studios. Mosaic tiles line the walls and the 23-karat gold leaf toilet, with its old-fashioned overhead pull chain, is set into the corner.*

LEFT: *A detail of the unpolished marble mosaic floor. The marble of Roman red, yellow, and white has retained its color through the years.*

OPPOSITE: *An Empire-style gilt cabinet hangs over the tub. Brass pipes run around the perimeter of the room, complementing the golden tones of the room.*

Roman red, yellow, gold, and white, along with a brass trim for pipes, doors, door facings, and the accessory rack.

All the wooden surfaces, including the window frame and shutters, standing cabinet, water tank, and toilet seat and lid, were gilded with twenty-three-karat gold leaf. A small footbath fits perfectly between the tub and the toilet along one wall.

Sunlight streams in through a magnificent stained-glass window attributed to Tiffany Studios. A Victorian brass fireplace with a Louis XV–style screen stands on one wall of the room. In addition to the two intricately hammered brass chests that serve as medicine cabinets, the bath door itself is wrapped in a unique buttoned brass design, evoking the vibrant style that Alice Whitridge Garrett brought to each room of this very special house.

ABOVE LEFT: *The footbath surround is gilded with 23-karat gold leaf. The footbath is at the foot of the tub, separating it from the toilet.*

LEFT: *The toilet seat—like all the wooden surfaces—was finished in gold leaf.*

OPPOSITE, ABOVE: *The fireplace is flanked by a cartouche-shaped Victorian brass screen of mesh and ormolu. A Federal Giltwood mirror portraying an idyllic painted scene is above the marble sink, and thin brass rods hold hand towels.*

OPPOSITE, BELOW: *A detail of the waste lever at the head of the tub.*

DESIGNER: HERTER BROTHERS (1885)

CONTRACTOR: CHARLES L. CARSON

FLOOR: MARBLE MOSAIC TILE

WALLS: MARBLE MOSAIC TILE

TUB: 23-KARAT GOLD LEAF

SINK: MARBLE

TOILET: 23-KARAT GOLD LEAF

LIGHTING: ANTIQUE

TUB FITTINGS: ANTIQUE

SINK FITTINGS: ANTIQUE

WASTEBASKET: ANTIQUE PORCELAIN

White Shades

Designer Jeffrey Bilhuber converted a bedroom, bathroom, and sewing room into a generous bath and dressing room in this Bucks County, Pennsylvania, weekend house. The owners' wish list for the new bathroom was fairly straightforward: "neutral colors and nothing overly ornate." Although the owners were quite adamant about having no color in the room, Bilhuber actually incorporated more than a dozen shades of white to give it depth and form, and to serve as a backdrop for the assemblage of English, French, and Russian antiques that fill the bath and dressing room area.

The design's serene and discreet point of view is derived from Bilhuber's approach to the finished bath. "The domestic level has been addressed," he explains. "There's real furniture here that exists in a furnished room similarly to the way it does throughout the rest of the house."

For example, twin travertine marble sinks are set into nineteenth-century bamboo chests that came from the

TOP RIGHT: *The dressing table is framed by two of the six oversized windows that flood the room with light.*

CENTER RIGHT: *A pull-out panel, adjacent to the closet doors, can discreetly accommodate an extensive collection of shoes. Springbok horns serve as pulls.*

RIGHT: *The walk-in closet is located opposite the dressing table. A collection of hatboxes adds a sense of style to the space.*

OPPOSITE: *A 19th-century bamboo chest is used as a dressing table in this Pennsylvania weekend house. A tortoiseshell mirror rests on the table; a rustic basket is placed underneath for waste.*

couple's previous home. Enameled in a creamy white, the drawers beneath pull out for extra storage. The third chest functions as a dressing table and is set in the middle of the room against a mirrored wall, with a tortoiseshell mirror dating from the early nineteenth century as its focal point.

Light, one of the greatest luxuries (especially in a bath), comes from myriad sources, but six oversized windows provide natural light all day long. And to make the most of them, Bilhuber added cafe curtains in a soft fabric that covers only two thirds of the window.

Four eighteenth-century French chairs are covered in an Indian silk check on one side, with a sheer cotton mosquito netting from China Seas on the other side. These can be moved around the room as the need arises, allowing sunlight to stream through their silhouettes. A worn cotton carpet from Stark underfoot contributes to the room's furnished feeling.

With furniture and objects from the eighteenth to the twentieth centuries, Bilhuber has established a quiet timelessness in this bath.

ABOVE: *The owner's assortment of framed nudes complements the 18th-century Italian sconce above the tub. The surround is extra deep for sponges and soaps and bath oils.*

LEFT: *A close-up of the unfilled travertine marble that surrounds the sink, with a soapstone dish.*

OPPOSITE, ABOVE: *The Louis XVI chair is upholstered in a translucent slipcover of Indian silk with a backing of mosquito netting.*

OPPOSITE, BELOW: *The toilet is enclosed in a separate closet, with a Queen Anne—style mirror, dating from the forties, over its sink of cream marble. Lighting is provided overhead and by Russian 19th-century silver-plated candlestick lamps.*

DESIGNER: JEFFREY BILHUBER, BILHUBER, INC.

FLOOR: EBONY STAINED WOOD; STARK CARPET

TUB: KOHLER

SINK: KOHLER

SHOWER: KOHLER

TOILET: KOHLER

LIGHTING: 18TH-CENTURY ITALIAN SCONCES; 1940'S OVERHEAD TOLE LIGHTING

Connecticut Fantasy

Michael Trapp, an antiques dealer of garden and architectural artifacts, is also well known as a garden designer and decorator. He lives above his charming shop in a rambling Greek Revival house in West Cornwall, Connecticut, a small village in the northwestern corner of the state. Several years ago he undertook a major renovation of the bath area, with the help of his caretaker, David Duvier Kuehn.

A wall was removed, as was a staircase. A window and a tub were added, and storage cupboards, a vanity, and a window seat were built from the architectural pieces and orphaned fragments that find their way to Trapp's shop.

The result is a lushly romantic room

ABOVE RIGHT: *A view of the tub and the love seat, with a massive urn in between. The floor, from France, is 18th-century Parquet de Versailles and is bordered with peg tile.*

RIGHT: *Four old doors, washed white, are the bases for the sink area. The owner added three pieces of old marble to form the sink surround and hung a gilt-framed mirror above.*

OPPOSITE: *A 19th-century tin tub from France is center stage beneath the sun-filled window with its elaborate backdrop of draped linen sheets.*

ABOVE: *A detail of the marble sink. The brass fixtures are a find from the owner's shop.*

OPPOSITE: *Dried flowers hang upside down on the horizontal wainscoting behind the old-fashioned white toilet.*

DESIGNER: MICHAEL TRAPP

CONTRACTOR: STAN DZNEUTIS

FLOOR: 18TH-CENTURY PARQUET DE VERSAILLES, BORDERED WITH PEG TILES

WALLS: FRENCH AND VICTORIAN FRAGMENTS

TUB: 19TH-CENTURY FRENCH

SINK: 19TH-CENTURY AMERICAN

SHOWER: 19TH-CENTURY ENGLISH PEG TILES; SLABS OF BLACK MARBLE

TOILET: ORIGINAL TO HOUSE

FITTINGS: ANTIQUE

TOWEL BAR: ANTIQUE

TOWELS/LINENS: POTTERY BARN

accessorized by the myriad objects acquired by this inveterate collector. A nineteenth-century tin tub from France sits beneath a window framed by antique linen sheets, dried tuber roses, and Spanish moss. "The tub had to be deep enough and long enough for those hot soaks that I adore," Trapp says.

The floor, originally from France but discovered by Trapp in St. Louis, is of eighteenth-century Parquet de Versailles. An entire wall built from bits and pieces of French and Victorian cottage windows and doors now houses the linen cupboard. Trapp painted it a "dirty Pompeian red" and filled it with stacks of old linens, towels, and bathroom necessities. "I collect old linens," he explains. "I love stacks of beautiful, clean, crisp, and orderly linens. And the contrast with the worn, weathered pieces in this room is perfect—each shows the other off to its greatest advantage, giving it all an old-world feeling."

Adjacent to the tiled shower stall sits the old sink with its antique brass fixtures. A friend had the Victorian basin and marble counter and Trapp simply added pieces at either end to make it fit his space. The toilet is original to the house, but the designer added the American Empire molding around the perimeter of the room.

A room that looks as if it might have been here forever, the bath actually took Trapp only three months to pull together. "It all fell into place ... everything seems to be the way it should be."

An Innovative Classic

"I loved the look of the original bathroom—the old marble sinks with glass legs, the glass-block shower, which was probably very avant-garde at the time it was done. We wanted to keep all the old fixtures and decorate the space so that it would have a quiet elegance," recalls one of the owners of the tranquil bath found in a three-story stone manor house in Greenwich, Connecticut.

The bath is located between the elegant master bedroom suite and the his-and-hers dressing rooms. The owners worked closely with designer Victoria Hagan, agreeing that they "wanted the bathroom to relate to the look of the master bedroom, but at the same time be functional."

Fortunately, not a great deal of renovation was required of this room, which had remained largely unchanged since the house was built in 1940. In fact, the renovation was primarily done to bring back the original look of the bath. A half wall was built between the bath and the toilet to separate them, but the original glass-block shower remained untouched.

The celadon wallpaper from the London firm of Osborne & Little not only echoes the coloration of Long Island Sound, which this room looks out onto, but also provides the perfect backdrop for the bold metal accessories, including a stool and basket from the shop Sentimento, that accentuate this bath.

"After a bathroom 'functions,' I think that accessories

The colors of this bathroom evoke the waters of nearby Long Island Sound. The white marble niche at the head of the tub holds bath supplies.

are most important to give the room its own personality," notes Hagan. And in keeping with that premise, a polished nickel storage shelf, from John Rosselli Ltd., holds a plethora of monogrammed towels, an antique silver-plated mirror and clock, silver jars, and a nickel dental cabinet with numerous drawers.

Because of its location, this bath is the beneficiary of wonderful natural light, and only minor changes were therefore required with regard to lighting. A brass chandelier, which has great sentimental meaning for the owners, was the only addition. Tubular lighting around the original mirror over the sink provides necessary task light.

Working closely together, the owners and the designer achieved not only the softly romantic room that they sought, but one that also works exceedingly well as a bathroom.

DESIGNER: VICTORIA HAGAN INTERIORS

FLOOR: ORIGINAL WHITE TILE; RUG, ELIZABETH EAKINS

WALLS: OSBORNE & LITTLE WALLPAPER

TUB: ORIGINAL

SINK: WHITE PORCELAIN IN WHITE MARBLE COUNTER

SHOWER: GLASS BLOCK ENCLOSED

TUB FITTINGS: DORNBRACHT

SHOWER FITTINGS: ORIGINAL

SINK FITTINGS: ORIGINAL

TOWELS/LINENS: ANICHINI

WASTEBASKET: SENTIMENTO, ANTIQUE FRENCH

STOOL: SENTIMENTO

ABOVE LEFT: *The glass-brick shower with its curved wall is original to the house. The plain white tile floor is accented with an Elizabeth Eakins rug.*

ABOVE RIGHT: *A detail of the shower, with a chrome dish for shower paraphernalia.*

RIGHT: *A bath caddy from Czech & Speake holds sponges and supports the bath mirror.*

OPPOSITE, ABOVE: *A wicker basket holds washcloths on the marble-topped double sink. Antique crystal jars line the counter above the sink.*

OPPOSITE, BELOW: *The original double sink is glass-legged and is topped by a slab of marble.*

Unabashedly Feminine

San Francisco fashion designer Jessica McClintock adores furniture and accessories with the patina of age. In her house overlooking San Francisco Bay and the Golden Gate Bridge, she wanted "every room to be a jewel box."

The bath in her master bedroom suite most definitely achieves that aspiration. In McClintock's own words, she designed the bath to be a "magical place—the antithesis of the modern, glossy bath." The bathroom space itself was originally a bedroom before its renovation fifteen years ago.

With its massive yet graceful bathtub—two Victorian-era tubs cut in half and joined together with a hand-carved casing—the McClintock bathroom emanates the elegance that is the trademark of her fashion design. A large pale pine armoire with hand-carved details and a mirror adds to this feminine ambience, as do the oval etched glass doors, which disguise the shower and the toilet. But the centerpiece of McClintock's bath, which she created with designer Diane Burns-Eden, is certainly the sumptuous dressing table with

A hand-blown Venetian glass chandelier is suspended above the elegant dressing table draped in Battenberg and Irish lace.

121

its softly worn Battenberg and diaphanous Irish lace, antique crystal jars, carved kingwood and walnut mirror, bottles, and bowls. A bust of a young French girl and an ever-present cluster of roses complete the decor. "I always have lots of flowers in my life," McClintock says.

Generous natural light streams in during the daytime, augmented by the ornate Venetian glass chandelier. Arched doorways and unusually high ceilings further enhance the drama of this private retreat. And the exquisite attention to detail—the antique handles and knobs, the old linens and lace, the hand-painted walls and floors—evokes the European intimacy that McClintock sought.

ABOVE LEFT: *The serpentine curved design of washed pine atop the shower door is repeated throughout the room.*

LEFT: *A detail of the painted floor.*

OPPOSITE: *Two Victorian-era tubs have been cut in half and rejoined to create this massive but graceful bathtub. The ever-present roses stand next to the tub.*

ABOVE LEFT: *Antique crystal jars and bottles stand on the dressing table, brightened by generous natural light.*

ABOVE: *Two cherubs frolic beside a lace-covered chair next to the tub and a double towel rack.*

LEFT: *An oval mirror graces the large pale pine armoire notable for its hand-carved details. Curved glass doors on either side provide see-through storage.*

OPPOSITE, ABOVE: *A bust of a young French girl and an ornate mirror dominate the dressing table.*

OPPOSITE, BELOW: *The pedestal sink is placed strategically in front of a painted mantelpiece and the mirror that has been affixed to the wall. An elaborate pair of sconces flanks the sink.*

ARCHITECT: TED EDEN

DESIGNER: DIANE BURNS-EDEN

CONTRACTOR: BOB GUNNELL CONSTRUCTION

FLOOR: PAINTED, AMY MCGILL

TUB: BILL SULLIVAN, CUSTOM

LIGHTING: HAND-BLOWN VENETIAN GLASS
  CHANDELIER

TUB FITTINGS: P. E. GUERIN

Theatrical Splendor

"Splendid whimsy," in the words of designer Michael de Santis, is an apt description for the over-the-top bathroom of Martin Richards, the producer of many films and Broadway plays, including the musicals *Sweeney Todd*, *La Cage aux Folles*, and *Grand Hotel*.

Richards's bath is located on the lower level of a maisonette apartment overlooking the East River in Manhattan. To create the luxurious space, de Santis choreographed a total renovation, including new marble floors, walls, and lighting.

The inspiration for the master bath came, de Santis recalled, from the notion of "a private folly reminiscent of the fanciful rooms set designer and architect

ABOVE RIGHT: *The marble-walled shower with fixtures by Sherle Wagner. Two triangular marble inserts hold shower essentials.*

RIGHT: *The owner's initials are carved in the bath's tentlike ceiling—cast in spheres and laurel wreaths—inspired by the imperial campaign tents of Alexander the Great and Napoleon.*

OPPOSITE: *The ornate and elaborate tub in the New York City bathroom of theatrical and film producer Marty Richards. Ridged steps flank both sides of the tub.*

Joseph Urban might have created for the great Ziegfeld." Since there were space limitations (no expansion was feasible), de Santis achieved the desired effect through a careful selection of elegant materials, a devotion to detail, and "a rich imagination."

The tentlike ceiling—evocative of French Directoire campaign tents—sets the tone for the room. Its motifs include a cast laurel wreath and spears, with Richards's cipher as the centerpiece. Lavish fixtures from the Kohler Company and Sherle Wagner and a carved gold-leafed wall reinforce the "luxe" ambience of the room. Classical Hellenistic and Roman iconography carved in the glass shower and water closet doors complete the "splendid panache" that de Santis set out to deliver.

DESIGNER: MICHAEL DE SANTIS

CONTRACTOR: JOHN RICHEDA, THE
    CREATIVE CORE

FLOOR: PRECISION STONE

WALLS: PAINTED BY DENNIS ABBE

TUB: PRECISION STONE

SINK: CHRISTINE BELFOR DESIGN LTD.

SHOWER: PRECISION STONE

TOILET: KOHLER

FITTINGS: SHERLE WAGNER

TOWEL BAR: SHERLE WAGNER

TOILET TISSUE HOLDER: SHERLE WAGNER

HOOKS: SHERLE WAGNER

TOWELS/LINENS: DAVID FORSTER & COMPANY

WASTEBASKET: DENNIS ABBE; CUSTOM

ABOVE: *Mirrored doors conceal ample storage space. The diagonal pattern on the marble floor serves to visually increase the size of the space.*

OPPOSITE, ABOVE: *Behind the mirrors, towels are stacked on shelves. Even the hidden drawers and insides of the doors are elaborately embellished with gold painted designs.*

OPPOSITE, BELOW: *The walls of the water closet are covered with a military blue and gold stripe.*

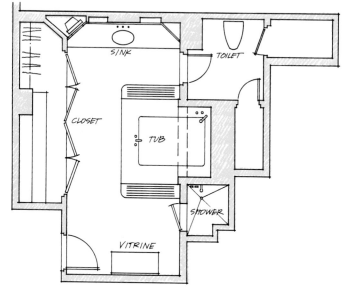

Nostalgic

*Reflecting
the ambience of an
earlier time*

Maugham Memories

The Los Angeles home of film director George Cukor was a gathering place for many of the actors, actresses, and writers with whom he worked during his illustrious career. For instance, in the 1920s, Somerset Maugham lived in the ground-floor guest room of the Cukor home while he completed the screen adaptation of his novel *The Razor's Edge.*

The present-day owners, Lynn von Kersting and her husband, Richard Irving, have attempted, in her words, "to keep the home fires burning for the romance and easy glamour of the old Hollywood colony." This commitment is clearly evident in their design of the cabana bathroom in the room that Maugham occupied.

The room itself, although only ten feet by ten feet, comfortably contains all the necessary elements and more for a cabana-cum-bathroom. It also succeeds in retaining the spirit and atmosphere of the small studio that Maugham wrote in.

Von Kersting chose a large banana-leaf wallpaper that was originally made for the Beverly Hills Hotel in the 1930s; it echoes the fronds of banana trees growing outside the casement windows and makes excellent use of the small space. A built-in window seat and adjoining cabinets line the outside wall; opposite, von Kersting has added a few choice pieces of pale celadon French wicker from the '30s.

This evocative cabana bathroom in Los Angeles is filled to the rafters with Maugham memorabilia and artifacts from the south of France. The original sink is skirted with a snappy cabana-stripe canvas.

DESIGNER: LYNN VON KERSTING FOR INDIGO SEAS

FLOOR: ORIGINAL BEACH CLUB CEMENT

WALLPAPER: INDIGO SEAS

SINK: ORIGINAL

SHOWER: ORIGINAL, SPEAKMAN SHOWERHEAD

TOILET: KOHLER

SHOWER FITTINGS: ORIGINAL AMERICAN STANDARD

TOWELS/LINENS: INDIGO SEAS

SHOWER CURTAIN: INDIGO SEAS, 1930S FRENCH WOODEN BEAD CURTAIN

PAINTINGS, ANTIQUES, AND FABRIC: INDIGO SEAS

ABOVE LEFT: *Outside the casement window are fronds of banana trees while inside, the designer lined the walls of the bath with banana-leaf wallpaper, originally made for the Beverly Hills Hotel in the 1930s.*

BELOW LEFT: *French 1930s wicker fills the room in front of the original toilet. A swinging wooden door provides privacy, while antique beads do the same for the shower.*

OPPOSITE: *A stack of books by Maugham make a comfortable connection to the past.*

Seaside Retreat

At Caroline Hirsch's home on the East End of Long Island (see pages 59, 159), designer Glenn Gissler created a bathroom adjacent to the large swimming pool that overlooks Mecox Bay. Guests use this bath to shower and change after swimming.

The bathroom has a simple, straightforward design. An apple-green wooden hamper adds some color to the clean white lines of the room, and in keeping with the same neutral tones, the French limestone tile floor is a soft beige color. The lighting supplements the ample natural light.

The view out the window offers privacy, thanks to the abundance of mature pine trees, but shades are also provided for less bold houseguests. These old-fashioned pull-down shades complement the Shaker wooden pegs for towels and swimsuits.

ARCHITECT: FRANCIS FLEETWOOD

DESIGNER: GLENN GISSLER DESIGN, INC.

FLOOR/SHOWER: FRENCH LIMESTONE

WALLS: BATTEN-BOARD

SINK: BELLE EPOQUE

SHOWER: DISTINCTIVE SHOWER DOORS

TOILET: AMERICAN STANDARD

FIXTURES: URBAN ARCHAEOLOGY

TOWELS/LINENS: RALPH LAUREN HOME
   COLLECTION

HAMPER: COMING TO AMERICA

ABOVE RIGHT: *The bath opens onto the pool and the bay, with a wooden deck connecting the two.*

BELOW RIGHT: *The pedestal sink, although newly made, fits in perfectly with the mood of the room, while the step-up shower is boxed within its own stall.*

OPPOSITE: *Batten-board walls painted an off-white suggest early seaside architecture.*

Ranch House Restoration

When Los Angeles designer Karin Blake and her husband, Bill Levine, bought this retreat in the heart of Montana ranch country, it presented her with a different decorating challenge than she usually faces in her bicoastal design projects. Here, she was working primarily with logs, as she and her son Justin—along with Peter Marbanian, a contractor she had previously worked with—set out to recapture the turn-of-the-century origins of Crow Hollow Ranch.

The original bathroom in the house was small, so Blake opted to convert one of the second-floor bedrooms into a new bathroom, retaining its plank flooring. The wall chinking was repaired, with special care being taken to highlight the existing rough-hewn beams. Blake moved the claw-

ABOVE RIGHT: *The antique medicine cabinet complements this simple, but painstakingly undertaken, restoration.*

RIGHT: *A close-up of the tub's faucet and drain.*

OPPOSITE: *The rough-hewn beams that line the wall, along with the claw-foot tub, succeed in suspending time in this Montana farmhouse. The stool was found in a local shop.*

DESIGNER: KARIN BLAKE

CONTRACTOR: PETER MARBANIAN

FLOOR: ORIGINAL PLANK FLOORS

WALLS: ROUGH-HEWN BEAMS

TUB: ANTIQUE CLAW-FOOT TUB

SINK: CRANE

TOILET: BRIGGS, ORIGINAL

TOWEL RACK: YELLOWSTONE RIVER ANTIQUES

TOWELS/LINENS: RALPH LAUREN HOME
    COLLECTION

foot toilet from the old bath into the new space and imported new fixtures and materials—some of which she carried on the plane from Los Angeles.

The claw-foot tub, which was shipped to the Montana house from California, takes center stage in this renovation. Blake accessorized the bath with objects that reinforce the ambience of the original ranch house. An old medicine cabinet was discovered in an antiques shop in Bozeman, Montana; a stool came from a shop in Livingston, Montana; and a Shaker-style red barrel was transported from Maine and recycled into a hamper. The vintage robes that Blake collects hang from an antique towel rack and further enhance the return of the ranch house to its roots.

ABOVE: *Simple mason jars are used as containers for bathroom necessities such as cotton balls and Q-tips. The wall chinking was repaired.*

RIGHT: *The designer chose to subtract, rather than add, in the bath's restoration. The simplicity of the planked floors and door complements the slanted walls.*

OPPOSITE: *The owner's passion for fly-fishing is reflected in this wood carving on the bathroom door.*

Pure White

The pristine white tones and sleek minimalist accessories of this design evoke the bathrooms of an earlier era. Created by Vicente Wolf in a prewar Upper West Side apartment building in New York City, this bath is blessed with the height common to apartments in that area.

To develop a retro, oversized scale, Wolf added a ten-foot-high terry-cloth shower curtain and retained such old details as the round towel bar and the glass doorknobs. As Wolf notes, "The client wanted the respectability of an old bathroom, but with all the easy maintenance of a new one." Completing the style of this seamless white bath is a black-and-white silver-print photograph taken by Louise Dahl-Wolfe and set in a modern white frame, casually propped against the window.

DESIGNER: VICENTE WOLF ASSOCIATES, INC.

CONTRACTOR: PAUL BAVOSA

FLOOR/WALLS: AMERICAN OLEAN

TUB/SINK: ANTIQUE

TOILET: AMERICAN OLEAN

LIGHTING: MSK

SINK FITTINGS: ANTIQUE

TOWEL BAR: ANTIQUE

TOWELS/LINENS: PRATESI

SHOWER CURTAIN: VICENTE WOLF ASSOCIATES, INC.

ABOVE LEFT: *The terry-cloth shower curtain complements the pure-white feeling that the designer has created. The floor is a clean white tile from American Olean.*

LEFT: *A black-and-white photograph from the '40s is one of the few accessories in the bath and subtly recalls an earlier time.*

OPPOSITE: *The pedestal sink was original to this 1930s New York City bathroom. The frosted glass window—common in city apartments—offers light and privacy.*

His/Hers

Creative

and compatible

approaches

Urban Harmony

When the last of Peri Wolfman and Charley Gold's four sons left for college in 1990, the couple set out to reinvent their living space in a large loft space located in downtown Manhattan. Both came to the project with considerably more than a layperson's knowledge of bathrooms. Charley is a still-life photographer, and Peri is the owner of Wolfman–Gold & Good Company, a shop well known for its collection of unique items for the home; together, they have also published design books.

They divided the loft—a full floor in the building—into two sections. One half houses Charley's studio and the other half is devoted to the couple's living space. Starting with essentially raw space, the couple constructed two bathrooms off

ABOVE LEFT: *A bead and batten wall, with crown moldings atop, divides the tub from the rest of the room.*

LEFT: *Natural elements include a basket with soaps, sponges, a loofah, and a body brush.*

OPPOSITE: *The elegant lines of the porcelain pedestal sink form the centerpiece in Peri Wolfman's bath. The mirror, made of antique brass, is situated so that natural light is available for makeup application.*

their bedroom, one for Peri, the other for Charley. Based on similar design themes, each features large windows and the materials that were common to buildings at the turn of the century, such as wainscoting, pedestal sinks, brass fittings, and marble sink counters.

The accessories differentiate Peri's bathroom from Charley's. Hers has antique crystal and silver bottles and silver-handled makeup brushes; his, slightly more spare, contains bottles of cologne and silver-handled hairbrushes. A charming old pie safe in Charley's bath holds extra washcloths and soaps. Both bathrooms have baskets with lids for hiding shampoo bottles and accessories; there are also baskets filled with white towels and others filled with rolls of toilet paper. Each room has its distinct personality, but each also attains the ambience the couple sought: calm, comfortable, and very functional.

ABOVE LEFT: *The medicine chest is hidden behind a gilt-framed mirror.*

OPPOSITE: *An antique pie safe does double duty: It holds soaps and towels and it displays some of Charley Gold's collections.*

HERS

ARCHITECT: LARRY BOGDANOW

DESIGNERS: WOLFMAN, GOLD, AND BOGDANOW

CONTRACTOR: PETER CODELLA

FLOOR: 8" WIDE PINE, PAINTED

WALLS: PAINTED WAINSCOTING

SINK: VINTAGE PEDESTAL

SHOWER: AMERICAN OLEAN

TOILET: AMERICAN STANDARD

TUB FITTINGS: PHYLRICH

SHOWER FITTINGS: PHYLRICH

SINK FITTINGS: GEORGE TAYLOR

SHOWER CURTAIN: WHITE DUCK, WOLFMAN–GOLD & GOOD CO.

HIS

ARCHITECT: LARRY BOGDANOW

DESIGNERS: WOLFMAN, GOLD, AND
BOGDANOW

CONTRACTOR: PETER CODELLA

FLOOR: WALNUT WOOD, AMERICAN OLEAN
WHITE

WALLS: PAINTED WAINSCOTING

SHOWER: AMERICAN OLEAN

TOILET: AMERICAN STANDARD

LIGHTING: VINTAGE BRASS SCONCES WITH
FROSTED FLAME GLASS

TUB FITTINGS: PHYLRICH

SHOWER FITTINGS: PHYLRICH

SINK FITTINGS: GEORGE TAYLOR

SHOWER CURTAIN: WHITE DUCK,
WOLFMAN–GOLD & GOOD CO.

ABOVE: *His marble sink surround has an overlip to keep water splashes in the sink. The faucet is attached directly to the wainscoted wall behind.*

RIGHT: *Every inch of space in his bath has been designed with an eye toward economical storage, from the enamel-covered wire basket system to the wicker storage baskets.*

OPPOSITE, ABOVE LEFT: *His toilet area is raised up from the rest of the room, with wainscoted walls and a tile floor.*

OPPOSITE, BELOW LEFT: *A plethora of paper in a grapevine basket.*

OPPOSITE, BELOW RIGHT: *Classic tiles line the walls of the shower.*

Country Relations

Advertising agency executives Candy and Keith Green moved several years ago from their loft in New York's Greenwich Village to a large house in Old Lyme, Connecticut. This was not the well-traveled road to the suburbs that many New Yorkers take but rather a move to a classic New England village, a 250-year-old town known as the birthplace of American Impressionism.

The couple's decision to create a distinct bath for each of them was based both on the availability of the space and on the fact that they married as adults and had each come to cherish privacy. A hallway leads from the master bedroom to the two bathroom/dressing rooms, with velvet drapes serving as "doors" to each.

Candy's bathroom is decidedly feminine, with soft linen drapes, subtle pink-and-white-striped wallpaper, and a graceful chandelier. Accessories include her collections of American pottery and antique beaded bags.

Keith's bathroom, on the other hand, captures the feel of a turn-of-the-century man's private dressing room. Whereas

Keith has a separate shower stall, framed in mahogany wood, in the center of his bathroom, which also contains a marble sink and built-in shelves.

HIS

DESIGNER/CONTRACTOR: KEITH GREEN

FLOOR: FIR

MAHOGANY: GENERAL WOODCRAFT

WALLS: ROBERT ALLEN FABRIC

SINK: KOHLER

SHOWER: ULTRAVALVE, SPECIAL DIGITAL THER-
   MOMETER; STATVALVE, MEMORY PLUMBING
   PRODUCTS

WHIRLPOOL: EPIC

LIGHTING: ANTIQUE LAMPS

PLUMBING FITTINGS: DAVIS AND WARSHOW

TUB FITTINGS: BROADWAY

SHOWER FITTINGS: KOHLER, SPEAKERMAN
   SHOWERHEAD

SINK FITTINGS: KOHLER

TOILET TISSUE HOLDER: BALDWIN BRASS

HOOKS: BALDWIN BRASS

Candy sees her bathroom as a place of refuge and retreat, Keith looks at his as a place for cleansing and rejuvenation. Even Keith's selection of lighting serves to differentiate his space from Candy's, featuring a combination of overhead lighting, mirror lighting, and lamps. He notes that "the balance of lamplight along with the traditional bathroom lighting makes the room feel like a real room, not a bathroom."

ABOVE RIGHT: *Every detail was thought out in advance in this bath/dressing room, including the mirrored door panels. The lamp is part of the owner's extensive rooster collection.*

BELOW RIGHT: *A digital device from UltraValve controls the temperature and stream of water in the marble and glass shower.* ·

OPPOSITE, ABOVE LEFT: *A side view of his glass-enclosed shower stall.*

OPPOSITE, ABOVE RIGHT: *Keith designed and built the wall unit opposite the sink area.*

OPPOSITE, BELOW: *Belts and neckties are neatly organized on custom-designed bars in a corner opposite the shower.*

ABOVE: *A painted wall system follows the curve of Candy's bath, with a chintz pouf strategically placed for robes, towels, and clothing.*

LEFT: *Sunlight streams down onto the tub.*

OPPOSITE, ABOVE RIGHT: *To bring down the height of the ceiling and add warmth to the space, Candy designed the enclosed vanity area 20 inches lower than the ceiling.*

OPPOSITE, BELOW LEFT: *Some of her antique beaded bags hang on a brass hook next to the lace-paneled closet doors.*

OPPOSITE, BELOW RIGHT: *Looking into the vanity/sink area with its mirrored back wall and high-hat lights.*

HERS

DESIGNER/CONTRACTOR: KEITH GREEN

FLOOR: FIR

MAHOGANY: GENERAL WOODCRAFT

WALLS: RALPH LAUREN

TUB: EPIC

SINK: IMPORT, DAVIS & WARSHOW

SHOWER: ULTRAVALVE, SPECIAL DIGITAL THER-
MOMETER; STATVALVE, MEMORY PLUMBING
PRODUCTS

BIDET: GERBER

WHIRLPOOL: EPIC

LIGHTING: ANTIQUE LAMPS

PLUMBING FITTINGS: DAVIS AND WARSHOW

TUB FITTINGS: BROADWAY

SHOWER FITTINGS: KOHLER, SPEAKMAN
SHOWERHEAD

SINK FITTINGS: KOHLER

TOILET TISSUE HOLDER: BALDWIN BRASS

HOOKS: BALDWIN BRASS

Classic Companions

Caroline Hirsch, owner of Caroline's Comedy Club in New York City, built an authentic shingle-style home in eastern Long Island fronting both the Atlantic Ocean and Mecox Bay. For her bathroom, designer Glenn Gissler sought to produce, in his words, "the ultimate sybaritic retreat."

Located off the master bedroom, the bath is connected to the dressing room. It is flooded with natural light during the day (there are three windows overlooking the Atlantic) and has lamps plus recessed architectural lighting. The accessories are understated and elegant: antique silver lamps, antique silver jars and bottles, a tiny Tiffany clock, and, grouped over the tub, a collection of dramatic black-and-white photographs by Joe Andoe. Storage includes a recessed marble niche with shelves in the shower, plus numerous cabinets and drawers.

A soft upholstered chair, covered in a cozy chenille fabric, echoes the muted colors of the oriental Tabriz underneath. Beneath the rug are rectangular blocks of

Sunlight streams in through the windows of this unabashedly feminine bathroom overlooking the Atlantic Ocean; the large "vintage" whirlpool tub is from Kohler.

159

honed Carrara marble, chosen for their gently worn look. The bidet and toilet are placed discreetly to one side, and even the glass and nickel shower doesn't intrude on the room or its views.

Across the hall, a guest bath exudes a very masculine tone. Dark wood floors, a bentwood chair, and an antique mahogany washstand suggest the simple lines of an old-fashioned dressing room for men. To keep clutter at a minimum, recessed storage includes a rectangular niche in the marble-enclosed shower and a built-in medicine cabinet over the sink area.

The sense of serenity found in both baths is accomplished through the careful balancing of the views outside with an intelligent choice of texture, tones, and objects within.

ABOVE: *The toilet and the bidet sit discreetly to one side.*

ABOVE RIGHT: *The brushed-nickel shower enclosure has a seat and shelving—both built-in—and transom windows for steam release.*

OPPOSITE, ABOVE: *The polished nickel fixtures, old marble, and wainscoting add a turn-of-the-century ambience.*

OPPOSITE, BELOW: *A slab of marble runs across the sink area. Such touches as silver candlestick lamps and an upholstered stool add a certain panache to the bath.*

HERS

ARCHITECT: FRANCIS FLEETWOOD

DESIGNER: GLENN GISSLER DESIGN, INC.

FLOOR: CARRARA MARBLE

WALLS/PAINT: DONALD KAUFMAN COLOR, CUSTOM

TUB: KOHLER

SINK: AMERICAN STANDARD

SHOWER: DISTINCTIVE SHOWER DOORS

TOILET: AMERICAN STANDARD

BIDET: AMERICAN STANDARD

WAINSCOTING: PAINTED BEAD-BOARD

FITTINGS: HARRINGTON BRASS WORKS

TOWEL BAR: URBAN ARCHAEOLOGY

TOILET TISSUE HOLDER: URBAN ARCHAEOLOGY

TOWELS/LINENS: RALPH LAUREN HOME COLLECTION

PHONE TABLE: ANN MORRIS ANTIQUES

RUG: ANTIQUE

HIS

ARCHITECT: FRANCIS FLEETWOOD

DESIGNER: GLENN GISSLER DESIGN, INC.

FLOOR: OAK, STAINED DARK

WALLS: PAINTED BEAD-BOARD WAINSCOTING

PAINT: DONALD KAUFMAN COLOR, CUSTOM

SINK: ST. THOMAS CREATIONS

SHOWER: DISTINCTIVE SHOWER DOORS

TOILET: ST. THOMAS CREATIONS

LIGHTING: MR16 DOWNLIGHTS; ANTIQUE
SCONCES WITH PAPER SHADES

SHOWER FITTINGS: HARRINGTON BRASS WORKS

SINK FITTINGS: HARRINGTON BRASS WORKS

TOWEL BARS: URBAN ARCHAEOLOGY

TOILET TISSUE HOLDER: URBAN ARCHAEOLOGY

HOOKS: CZECH & SPEAKE

TOWELS: RALPH LAUREN HOME COLLECTION

SHUTTERS: CUSTOM

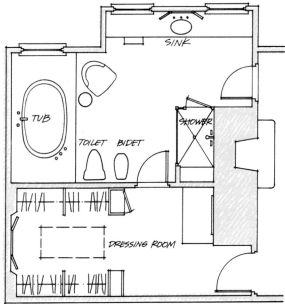

ABOVE LEFT: *The guest bathroom offers a view from the louvered window behind a wooden chair and circular shaving table. Mecox Bay and sand dunes appear as if in a painting.*

OPPOSITE: *Wainscoting is also used on the half wall that separates the toilet from the rest of the guest bathroom.*

Intrinsically Romantic

Designer Lynn von Kersting's renovation of the master baths in the California home of Pam and Bob Levin succeeds in evoking the allure of an earlier period. The renovation necessitated the transformation of the existing master bath into Bob Levin's bathroom, and the refiguring of a small library and closet into a bath suite for Pam.

The dominant theme in Pam Levin's bath is roses—they're found on the chair fabric, towels, and paintings, and the walls are glazed a pale rose color. A large oval-shaped tub is set into its own nook, and an oversized French mirror reflects sunlight from the garden. Large custom-built cabinets glazed in French apple-green tones provide storage space for bath paraphernalia. The unpolished travertine marble floor is laid on the diagonal and partially covered by a pale needlepoint rug.

In the renovation of Bob's bath, the original gray-tiled floor and walls were retained, and the walls above were glazed gray to match the tiles. Anglo-Indian balloon shades of faded claret and beige cover the original casement windows. A masculine touch is added by the collection of antique military paintings and prints. A nineteenth-century Chinese leather wedding box rests on a glass-fronted turn-of-the-century mahogany chest, and the much-in-evidence "RBL" monogrammed towels clearly establish this room as Bob's territory.

The mahogany chest at the end of Bob Levin's bathroom anchors the space. The Russian blue painted ceiling, with its detail of white molding, gives the room architectural strength, while the sturdy kilim-covered chair lends a note of masculinity.

HERS	
DESIGNER:	LYNN VON KERSTING FOR INDIGO SEAS
FLOOR:	MARBLE
WALLS:	STRIÉ
TUB:	MARBLE
SINK:	KOHLER
TOILET:	KOHLER
LIGHTING:	RECESSED, LAMPLIGHT
TUB FITTINGS:	CZECH & SPEAKE
SINK FITTINGS:	CZECH & SPEAKE
TOWELS/LINENS:	CUSTOM

HIS	
DESIGNER:	LYNN VON KERSTING FOR INDIGO SEAS
FLOOR:	TILE
WALLS:	STRIÉ
SINK:	AMERICAN STANDARD
SHOWER:	AMERICAN STANDARD
TOILET:	KOHLER
LIGHTING:	RECESSED
SINK FITTINGS:	CZECH & SPEAKE
SHOWER FITTINGS:	CZECH & SPEAKE
TOWELS/LINENS:	CUSTOM

ABOVE LEFT: *The gilt mirror in Pam Levin's bath reflects the striéd cabinetry and her collection of hat boxes.*

LEFT: *The room, with its painted cabinetry and Wedgwood pulls, contains treasures acquired on travels. Behind the louvered door on the left is the toilet.*

OPPOSITE: *Parisian salon curtains are hung over the French doors leading to the garden. A Moroccan pillow on a silk taffeta slipper chair from the 1920s completes this corner.*

Stylish

A suggestion of

luxe and an attention

to detail

Modern Reflections

The dictate given by the owner of this apartment on New York's Central Park to designer Vicente Wolf was to create a bath off the master bedroom that would "suggest the patina of age, yet not be overly decorated." A total renovation was required, which included the removal of fixtures dating back to 1905. In a period of eight months Wolf completed the project and garnered a judgment of "perfect" from the owner.

The designer divided the bathroom into two distinct areas, which he separated with a translucent green glass door. One area contains a toilet and sink, the other has the shower and a vanity, with its own sink. This design offers valuable flexibility, allowing the owner to create an extra powder room for overflow guests merely by shutting the glass door.

ABOVE LEFT: *The unframed glass shower door appears to float at one end of the bathroom.*

LEFT: *The black and white mosaic tile sparkles with flecks of gold mosaic interspersed throughout.*

OPPOSITE: *A slab of Thassos marble forms the sink surround in the outer room of this contemporary bath. The gooseneck fixture is by Kohler.*

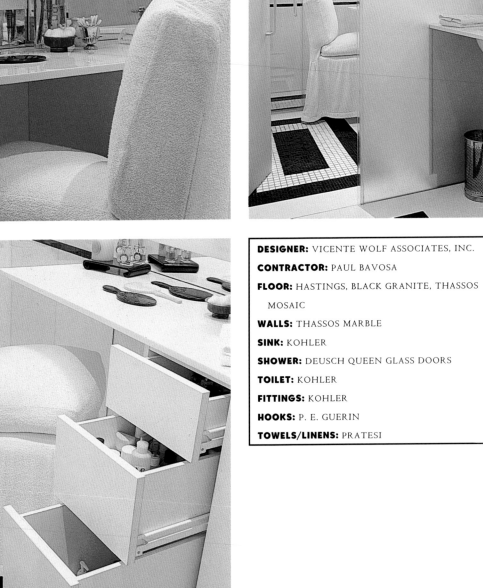

DESIGNER: VICENTE WOLF ASSOCIATES, INC.

CONTRACTOR: PAUL BAVOSA

FLOOR: HASTINGS, BLACK GRANITE, THASSOS
    MOSAIC

WALLS: THASSOS MARBLE

SINK: KOHLER

SHOWER: DEUSCH QUEEN GLASS DOORS

TOILET: KOHLER

FITTINGS: KOHLER

HOOKS: P. E. GUERIN

TOWELS/LINENS: PRATESI

A geometric black-and-white mosaic tile floor design unites the two separate parts of the bathroom and adds a touch of glamour. It also provides a visual contrast to the white vanity, with its slippered chair covered in practical terry cloth. Overhead recessed lighting complements the natural light from the small shower window.

Wolf used classic sink and shower fixtures from the Kohler Company. With two slabs of Thassos, the purest white marble, to create the sink surrounds, and a mirror of his own design over the vanity, he designed a sleek and stylish room.

ABOVE RIGHT: *The smoked glass door at one end of the shower provides privacy in this city bathroom. The step underneath serves as a shower seat.*

RIGHT: *Niches offer an end to shampoo clutter in the shower.*

OPPOSITE, ABOVE LEFT: *A close-up of the dressing-table area in the inner room. The Thassos marble continues as a counter, and terry-cloth covers the slipper chair.*

OPPOSITE, ABOVE RIGHT: *Smoked green glass divides the bath into two spaces, allowing it to function as a powder room for guests when the door is shut.*

OPPOSITE, BELOW: *Deep storage on roll-out drawers allows for easy access to a hair dryer, creams, and other bath necessities.*

Sophisticated Elegance

A long exterior hall connects a newly constructed bedroom, dressing room, and master bathroom to the rest of this country house located on Long Island's East End. Stephanie Stokes, who designed the interior of the house, used an assortment of techniques to achieve the calm and comfortable look her clients were seeking.

Limestone, rather than marble, was utilized for its informal feel. The limited color palette was based on a hand-blocked Christopher Hyland wallpaper full of muted cream and taupe tones; this inspired the bath's hand-painted striped wall. Burgundy monograms were added to the towels and a green marble border was used to frame the limestone floor in order to "jazz it up," Stokes says. A smart-looking green leather art deco stool was selected for the same reason.

The lighting is more than ample. From the vantage point of the whirlpool tub in the center of the room, light streams in from a central window above, as well as from two large windows at either end of the room, which overlook the private gardens. Additional lighting includes two sconces and valance lights over each washbasin; three overhead lights offer general illumination, and the shower area is lit by a wall-mounted ship's light.

Stokes ran the oversized wallpaper pattern above the freestanding walls as a design element to open up the room. Personal touches throughout—retro fixtures, read-

Limestone was used around the tub and on the vanity countertops of this sumptuous bath. A linen striped balloon shade hangs from the large windows overlooking the tub.

175

ABOVE LEFT: *Wooden lattice shelves allow air circulation in the linen closet.*

ABOVE: *Christopher Hyland's hydrangea-striped wallpaper adds elegance to the enclosed toilet.*

LEFT: *Next to the shower are oversized chrome hooks for post-shower terry-cloth robes. An art deco stool, covered in green leather, complements the color scheme of the room.*

OPPOSITE, ABOVE: *Closets line both sides of the hallway that leads from the bath area to the dressing area.*

OPPOSITE, BELOW: *Small sconces frame each of the vanities, and two chrome shelves and a magnifying mirror, hung on the wall, help relieve countertop clutter.*

ing racks, a jewelry holder placed alongside the washbasin, and plenty of hooks—make the space one of ease and comfort.

Generous storage space, one of Stokes's hallmarks in all of her projects, is provided not only by the numerous drawers under the two vanities for personal items but also by bath and shower racks. Towels and linens are stored in large closets, with wooden latticework shelves to ensure air circulation. The designer's skill in incorporating such details gives a sense of expansiveness to this sun-filled bath.

ARCHITECT/DESIGNER: STEPHANIE STOKES, INC.

ARCHITECTURAL, INTERIOR, AND CABINETRY DESIGN: BENJAMIN HUNTINGTON

CONTRACTOR: ARTHUR TRIFARI BUILDERS

FLOOR: SOUTHAMPTON MARBLE AND TILE, LIMESTONE AND MARBLE

WALLS: WALLPAPER, CHRISTOPHER HYLAND; FAUX PAINTING AND GESSO, BRIAN LEVER

SINK: KOHLER, CAXTON

SHOWER: ARCHITECTURAL DETAILS

TOILET: KOHLER

WHIRLPOOL TUB: KOHLER

STEAM: ARCHITECTURAL DETAILS

LIGHTING: JEROME SUTTER SCONCES, PELL ARTIFEX PENDANT LIGHTS

FITTINGS: ARCHITECTURAL DETAILS

TOWEL BAR: ARCHITECTURAL DETAILS

TOILET TISSUE HOLDER: ARCHITECTURAL DETAILS

TOWELS/LINENS: JOHN MATOUK & CO.

STOOL: HOWARD KAPLAN'S BATH SHOP

VANITY TOPS: LIMESTONE

Spatial Relations

Designer Vicente Wolf faced a formidable task in the renovation of this bathroom in a 1930s apartment on Manhattan's West Side, owned by Michael and Bonnie Pappadio. The project: to create one master bath out of two aging bathrooms that contained all the extraneous pipes and radiators and misallocated space so typical of that genre of New York City apartments. And, in the words of Bonnie Pappadio, Wolf succeeded brilliantly in "bringing our dreams to reality."

The bath is located off the master bedroom. With the sliding glass pocket door open, it works as a private master bath; with the door closed, it serves as a smaller powder room.

A mosaic floor was cleverly laid on an

ABOVE RIGHT: *A mahogany and gilt mirror, designed by Wolf, is lit by two incandescent tubes on either side, providing generous light for makeup and shaving.*

RIGHT: *A terry-cloth robe hangs on the door to the bedroom at one end of this L-shaped bathroom.*

OPPOSITE: *The diagonally arranged mosaic tile serves to visually increase the size of the shower area. The unframed glass shower doors reinforce the feeling of space.*

angle to visually increase the space. This complemented the mix of reclaimed 1930s fixtures and several pieces newly designed by Wolf to create a feeling of relaxed luxury. As Bonnie notes, "The space flows. It's luxurious with the illusion of a large space, and it's easy to maintain."

Lighting sources are myriad. There are high hats, lamps, incandescent lights around the mirrors, and strong natural light from the window. Accessories are kept to a minimum; they include an ivy topiary plant, a large wooden dish to hold Bonnie's makeup, and, on the wall, Andy Warhol's *Jackie* from the "Platinum Series."

Storage is both open and hidden. A six-foot-long, triple-tiered open cabinet, designed by Wolf and made of steel and marble, holds towels, magazines, and everyday needs, and a spacious floor-to-ceiling closet outfitted with numerous shelves provides ample storage for the overflow. Completing the design is a shower door made entirely of glass, with no metal seams, that takes up very little space visually in this well-designed bath.

DESIGNER: VICENTE WOLF ASSOCIATES, INC.

CONTRACTOR: PAUL BAVOSA

FLOOR: AMERICAN OLEAN

WALLS: DECORATOR WHITE, HIGH GLOSS

SINK: ANTIQUE

TOILET: KOHLER

SHOWER DOOR: DEUSCH QUEEN

LAMP: VICENTE WOLF

FITTINGS: KOHLER

TOWELS/LINENS: PRATESI

ABOVE: *Behind the sliding glass door is the second sink, which allows the room to function as an extra powder room for entertaining.*

ABOVE RIGHT: *A reflection in the mirror behind the small sink reveals the open pocket door with the larger sink beneath its mahogany and gilt mirror.*

OPPOSITE, ABOVE: *Concealed behind an unobtrusive door are seven shelves with ample storage space for bathroom needs. To the right is the sliding pocket door that can divide the bath into two rooms.*

OPPOSITE, BELOW: *Sunlight streams in on the Wolf-designed table for towels, books, and plants.*

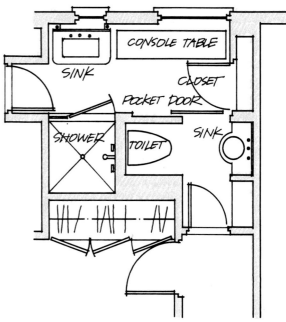

DESIGNER: VICTORIA HAGAN INTERIORS

FLOOR: EXISTING, BLACK MARBLE

WALLS: CUSTOM SLATE-BLUE WALLPAPER

SINK: EXISTING BLACK PEDESTAL, KOHLER

TOILET: EXISTING, KOHLER

LIGHTING: EVERGREEN ALABASTER DISH

SINK FITTINGS: EXISTING, BRASS

TOWEL BAR: URBAN ARCHAEOLOGY

TOWELS/LINENS: ANICHINI

WASTEBASKET: SENTIMENTO

ACCESSORIES: SENTIMENTO

BLINDS: WOOD

Shagreen Splendor

For a spacious stone Connecticut home, New York–based designer Victoria Hagan created a very feminine powder room, anchored by a large silver Venetian mirror that contrasts nicely with the modern slate sink underneath.

An outer room offers additional privacy. There, Hagan installed a small second sink of faux bamboo and marble, imparting a Victorian tone to the space. She added a small rectangular table covered in a soft celadon moiré fabric to display the owner's remarkable collection of shagreen.

ABOVE LEFT: *The owner's collection of shagreen and glass jars and bottles rests on a small dressing table.*

LEFT: *A modern slate and glass sink is juxtaposed with a Venetian glass mirror.*

OPPOSITE, ABOVE: *Old-fashioned fixtures complement the bathroom sink.*

OPPOSITE, BELOW: *A rectangular table has been fitted with celadon moiré. A classically simple window treatment allows the room to fill with light.*

Idyllic Design

When Lee and Howard Forman renovated the bathroom of their home in McLean, Virginia, they worked with designer Mary Douglas Drysdale to achieve, as Lee Forman expressed it, "the feeling of an idyllic living area."

They gutted both the original bath and the closets, reconfiguring the rooms and the roof to obtain the unusually high ceilings found in the bath/shower portion of the complex. A nine-month renovation resulted in a spacious and stylish new suite.

The room is divided into two distinct areas: one includes a nine-foot-long mirrored vanity, the tub, and a smaller vanity niche for applying makeup or drying hair, and the second is designed as a dressing area. Between them is the glass shower, a transparent bridge between the two spaces.

ABOVE RIGHT: *A nook has been built into one corner of the bathroom as a dressing table area. The mirrored walls have affixed makeup lights, while a silver tray holds hairbrushes and a hair dryer.*

RIGHT: *The tub is reflected in the late-19th-century armoire that is used for storage in the dressing area of the bath.*

OPPOSITE: *Glass bricks serve as sleek containers on the sink's countertop beneath the mirrored wall.*

Richly colored Chinese carpets partially cover the floor in both sections of the bathroom.

Although Howard is more of a traditionalist, Lee, a graphic designer known for her logos and stationery designs, prefers modern, sleek lines. Drysdale was able to merge these two different sensibilities. She added crown moldings and extensive chair railings to make the room slightly more traditional, and restructured the roof to accommodate the soaring ceiling. "It's a very architectural bath," notes Drysdale. "I tried to provide a sense of organization and coherence."

Because the longer vanity is built over the hall stairs, Drysdale raised the floor that leads to this room by several inches, increasing by the sense of entering a separate space. The toilet is enclosed in its own private room. Drawings depicting elements of different European buildings, executed by Chase Nelson, were commissioned especially for this room to complete the architectural theme.

DESIGNER: MARY DOUGLAS DRYSDALE,
   DRYSDALE DESIGN ASSOCIATES
FLOOR: TRAVERTINE MARBLE
WALLS: GIBSON WALL BOARD
SINK: KOHLER
SHOWER: CUSTOM
TOILET: AMERICAN STANDARD
WHIRLPOOL: AMERICAN STANDARD
LIGHTING: LIGHTOLIER
TUB/SINK FITTINGS: KROIN
SHOWER FITTINGS: GROHE
TOWEL BAR: KROIN
TOWELS/LINENS: PALAIS ROYALE

ABOVE: *The glass-enclosed shower does not intrude on the bathroom's design, yet is centrally located.*

OPPOSITE, ABOVE: *The large tub is set between two windows opposite the sink area. Architectural prints hang on the rich sand-toned walls, and the door on the left leads to the enclosed toilet.*

OPPOSITE, BELOW: *The mirrored wall adds to the open feeling; built-ins such as the cabinetry, drawers, and mirrored medicine cabinets at both ends of the sink area help reduce countertop clutter.*

Modern Pleasures

The client of designer Gary Hutton and architect Richard Brayton wanted a "luxurious, clean, contemporary look" in this master bath on the top floor of a house on Telegraph Hill in San Francisco.

The house, with a commanding view of the city below, was built in 1960. This present-day bathroom was originally two baths and two closets before Hutton and Brayton stepped in. Renovation was substantial—a year and a half's worth—but in Hutton's words, "It's now close to perfect, given the architectural restrictions." These constraints included the location of the elevator and the fact that no windows or exterior spaces could be added, due to code restrictions.

The goal was "to make a windowless bath into a space filled with natural light," and this was accomplished by adding three

ABOVE RIGHT: *Skylights overhead allow natural light to pour into the length of the room. The tub is situated on the left.*

RIGHT: *Unique storage cubes, with pull-out trays inside, are located under the double sinks and float on stainless-steel legs.*

OPPOSITE: *Beneath a wall of tile and mirror, the sinks are aqua-colored frosted glass.*

skylights in the room with a "pitched roof" design. The skylights allow natural light throughout the entire length of the bath, and the one over the tub actually opens to the sky, so one may shower or bathe "outdoors."

The tub, of lightweight concrete, and the undercounter cabinets were both designed by Brayton, and the Vitraform sinks were constructed of frosted glass. No special spa equipment was added, but the large tub allows for Japanese-style soaking. As a final touch, Hutton added a chaise longue in the master bedroom, next to the bath, for reading and relaxation.

ABOVE LEFT: *The skylight over the tub and shower area slides open for "outdoor" bathing.*

LEFT: *The bathroom features a custom free-standing concrete tub with a faucet by Kroin.*

OPPOSITE, ABOVE: *The tiles used on the walls are from Ann Sacks.*

OPPOSITE, BELOW: *The water closet is tile-lined and also topped with a skylight.*

ARCHITECT: RICHARD BRAYTON,
   BRAYTON & HUGHES, DESIGN STUDIO

DESIGNER: GARY HUTTON, GARY
   HUTTON DESIGN

CONTRACTOR: PARAGON
   CONSTRUCTION

FLOOR: SPANISH LIMESTONE

WALLS: ANN SACKS TILE AND STONE,
   CUSTOM

TUB: CUSTOM

SINK: CHERRY CREEK VITRAFORM

SHOWER: KROIN

TOILET/BIDET: AMERICAN STANDARD

FITTINGS: KROIN

TOWEL BAR: CUSTOM

TOILET TISSUE HOLDER: CUSTOM

HOOKS: KROIN

TOWELS/LINENS: CANNON

WASTEBASKET: ITALIAN STAINLESS
   STEEL

Resources & Inspiration

Today's Bathroom
Planning to Remodel
What the Pros Have to Offer
A Bathroom for All
Bathroom Planning Guidelines
Visual Resources
Architects and Designers Directory
Manufacturers Directory
Retail Outlets, Catalogs, Craftspeople, and More

Compiled by Kevin Clark

Today's Bathroom

Once relegated to a minor role in the design scheme of the home, the bath has now emerged as a pivotal room in the design of most residences. Along with the kitchen, it is the room that realtors consider most critical in establishing the market value of a home.

Remember, however, that the bathroom, as we know it, is a relatively recent phenomenon. It wasn't until the middle of the nineteenth century that people even had access to centrally sup-

Page 192: A turn-of-the-century outhouse restored for 20th-century use on a Montana ranch.
Above: Until recently, most baths did not reveal the attention to detail shown in the gold toilet of the Evergreen House bathroom, circa 1850.

plied water. Until then, water had to be brought by hand from a well or pump. With a few notable exceptions—such as the bath in Baltimore's Evergreen House, built in the 1850s—bathrooms were never the site of significant architectural or design interest.

The twentieth century introduced hot running water to our households, and new manufacturing technologies enabled companies like Kohler and American Standard to supply our homes with the bathtubs, sinks, and toilets that would come to be the foundation of the modern bathroom. But in creating this new space, design and architectural nuances continued to play a secondary role to function for most of the century. It was only with the convergence of homeowning affluence and design interest in the 1980s that the bathroom became a focal point for decorators, architects, and their clients.

What accounts for this new passion for the bath? Many observers note that with the often harried pace of life today, the bathroom offers a place of refuge not found anywhere else in the house. And it follows logically that for both personal and investment reasons, homeowners want to make this retreat as attractive as their space and budgets will allow. In addition, the growing popularity of spas both here and abroad has encouraged the development of home spas, with new products enabling us to re-create these settings using personal saunas, steam baths, and whirlpool baths.

At a more fundamental level, we are also a culture increasingly devoted to personal cleanliness. According to recent studies, the average American adult takes at least seven baths or showers a week, and 40 percent of women declare that their principal mode of relaxation is—you guessed it—taking a bath.

Architects and builders have responded to this interest by allocating more space and more design expertise to bathrooms in newly constructed houses. And bathroom designers, architects, and renovation experts have become skilled at reshaping existing bathroom spaces into more spacious, stylish, and exciting rooms.

In my search for great bathrooms, I discovered that no one design approach dominates today. Whether it was the nostalgic feel elicited by the wonderful pool house bath at the Hirsch house on the East End of Long Island, or the enchantingly romantic ambience of Jessica McClintock's San Francisco bath, or the over-the-top luxury offered by designer Michael de Santis for the New York apartment of producer Martin Richards, I was unfailingly inspired by the bathrooms that I photographed.

The purely functional approach toward baths espoused by earlier gener-

ations has been replaced by one that obviously still puts a premium on function but has tangibly and dramatically elevated the level of design. Decorators and architects now have access to a growing number of resources with which to create marvelous spaces. The availability of recessed lighting, for example, allows us to incorporate a sense of drama not available to our parents. And new developments in flooring, tiles, and window design add to the options available for shaping the look of our bathrooms.

The bath is an essential and important room in the house. To help balance our busy agendas, a stylish, idiosyncratic, or simply soothing bathroom can enhance our lives immeasurably. I hope that you will find the information you need here to create your own dream bathroom!

Left: Hooks and towel bars are located within arm's reach of the step-up marble shower in a stylish California bathroom.
Above: Elegant accessorization takes this small powder room in Lynn von Kersting's home to another level with its striéd walls, antique Venetian mirror, cinnabar vases overflowing with Moroccan rosemary, and Turkish and Moroccan prints and objets d'art.

Planning to Remodel

Before you remodel your bathroom, sit down and thoroughly plan what you want for yourself and your family. Be sure to resolve your expectations during the planning stages, not during construction or after the room is finished. This will save you a lot of aggravation and money. Mistakes are costly and in bathrooms, the fixtures—sink, tub, toilet, and shower stall—are placed to be permanent. In the living room, you can

The way it was: adult and child seats along with a rinsing bucket inside a rural Montana outhouse.

move a chair if you change your mind. In the bathroom, you cannot move the tub without spending considerable money.

Here are the steps to follow in the planning stage, before any work is done:
• Measure your bathroom and note the locations of the fixtures—tub, toilet, sink, and shower stall. Are you pleased with the locations? Is the circulation pattern in the room convenient and safe? Is there ample space for linen storage? Is your sink large enough to wash your hair? Is your towel bar located in a convenient spot? Is your

vanity large enough to hold all your toiletries? With a piece of graph paper and a straightedge, make a floor plan of the bathroom, using the ratio 1 inch equals 1 foot. This will avoid confusion and miscalculation. Show the overall size and shape of the space. Note the location of the doors, windows, skylights (if any), architectural elements (columns, fireplaces, built-ins), and fixtures.

• Take a piece of paper and divide it into two columns. Head one column Pluses, the other Minuses. On the plus side, list all the elements of your bathroom that you like. These can be anything from the wonderful turn-of-the-century fixtures to the convenient towel storage cabinet located next to the sink. On the minus side, list all the things about your bathroom that you don't like: chipped, stained, outdated, or ugly fixtures, unappealing tiles, cramped or inefficiently used space, or anything else that makes you cringe every time you enter the bathroom.

• Analyze the flaws and consider what could be done to correct them. Is the lighting poor? Is the tub located in an awkward spot? Is the room claustrophobic when you close the door?

• Decide what type of bathroom is appropriate for your lifestyle. Do you spend a lot of time bathing in the tub? Do you want a bathroom that can be a combination space—exercise

THE HUNT BEGINS:
HOW TO HIRE A CONTRACTOR

Finding a good contractor is not hard, if you know what to do and what to ask. Here are a few tips.

1. Ask friends and colleagues for recommendations. If you visit someone's home and admire a new bathroom, ask who did it.

2. When meeting a contractor, request references and ask to see some of the projects he or she has completed. Let the contractor explain the project. Talk to the people whose homes you visit and call the references the contractor gives you. Get information about a prospective contractor's background and personality. Remember, you will have this person practically living in your home for at least a few weeks.

3. Check the contractor's work schedule. If a contractor has seventeen other jobs, chances are your work will not begin in the near future.

4. Check the contractor's insurance and make certain that anybody he or she hires is insured. Injuries on the job do happen.

5. Insist on a written contract or agreement. Put everything in writing and leave nothing to chance. This avoids conflicts and arguments.

6. Ask lots of questions. Trust and communication are important. If you cannot talk to a contractor or do not understand what he or she wants to do no matter how many times it is explained to you, look elsewhere.

7. Convey your needs and expectations in as clear a manner as possible. After you have told the contractor what you want to do, ask for feedback to make sure that he or she understands the scope of the job. Ask for any suggestions that would make the project more efficient, cost-effective, and attractive.

room, dressing room, private retreat, spa? Do you have small children? Is your bathroom going to be a decorative powder room or is it the main bathroom for the entire family? Once you have decided what you want your bathroom to be, write it down.

- Lifestyle and taste work together to create the perfect bathroom for you. Decide what appeals to your sense of style but remember that trends come and go, so carefully consider color choices, fixture styles, and accessories before having them installed in your bathroom. Bear in mind that a home's resale value is strongly influenced by the bathroom. If your favorite color is, for example, blue, consider selecting neutral colored tiles and fixtures, and painting or wallpapering the walls blue. A potential buyer can easily envision painting or wallpapering the walls in another color, whereas a blue tub, toilet, and tiles might well discourage a sale.

- Based on your resources, carefully consider how much you can afford to spend. Determine a plausible maxi-

Surrounded by black, red, and white tiles, curved columns at either end of this beige bathtub hold red and white towels and bath paraphernalia.

mum amount. No matter how much you plan on spending, keep in mind that most renovations run 20 to 30 percent more than anticipated. Also, when you sell your house, you never fully recoup the total cost of the renovation; generally you can expect to recover approximately 75 to 80 percent, depending on the current market value of homes in your neighborhood.

• When renovating a bathroom, most people turn to a general contractor to execute their remodeling. But before he or she starts, you may wish to consult with an architect, interior designer, or certified bathroom designer. If you choose this route, speak to several candidates before making a decision. Bring your floor plan and your wish list to allow the professional to assess whether your ideas are viable and roughly how much they will cost. Do not be afraid to ask for references, review portfolios, and tour completed projects. An informed client is a happy client.

• Ask for the proposed budget in writing. This, in combination with such factors as personality, proximity to your home, and recommendations from previous clients, will help you decide whom to hire. Even after you have made your selection, do not be afraid to ask for revisions to your initial plan. Do not be forced into anything you do not want, and never become intimidated or discouraged. It is much easier to make changes on paper than during construction or after the job is completed. Also, be certain that the contractor does not rely solely on your floor plan for final budget and design. Most professionals will—and should—insist on visiting your home and doing their own floor plan and measurements before offering a budget. If yours does not, replace him or her.

• Before you let the professional begin, make certain that a timetable has been agreed upon and that the subcontractors are available to handle the work during that period. Be realistic and remember that every project runs into a minor snag or two, so allow yourself some extra time. Additionally, be sure that while work is being done on your bathroom you have another one available to you. If work is being done on your only bathroom, prepare to live somewhere else for a while. No matter how much you mentally prepare for in-house construction, you will feel displaced, invaded, and frustrated during the weeks it is going on. Don't despair. When all the work is completed, your dream bathroom will be a reality.

What the Pros Have to Offer

Using a professional architect to remodel your bathroom offers many benefits that can save you time, money, and mistakes. An architect knows which walls can be moved without compromising your structure and what needs to be done to remedy structural defects and flaws. He or she can arrange for a structural engineer to inspect the job and can manage the contractor and subcontractors. The architect can also provide the master plan that shows every step your renovation will take, including the installation of fixtures, electrical wiring, plumbing, and a list of materials and products to be ordered.

If you are planning major alterations or new construction that will alter the exterior of your home, you definitely need an architect. Plans for this type of work must be approved by the building department or planning commission in your community. To receive approval and a certificate of occupancy once the work is completed, you must submit certified working drawings containing the architect's seal, usually accompanied by an engineer's report. All drawings from the architect must be clear and explicit so the contractor has no problems in following and complying with them. Also, when doing any type of major construction, work permits must be applied for and then prominently displayed at the job site. Usually the contractor handles this paperwork.

Interior designers can also be used for bathroom design, but try to select

one who has years of experience in this particular area. A certified bathroom designer (CBD) or a bathroom design specialist can offer insights and expertise that a general contractor might not have and may be able to diagnose specific problems. A bathroom specialist should be able to assess your current

A painted landscape adds charm to this white bathroom, while double basin sinks with a long slab of granite in between and mirrored medicine cabinets help ease morning traffic.

bathroom, offer suggestions for better space utilization, and recommend products that will satisfy your needs. Finally, a bathroom specialist can help you review your budget and make smart choices about where your money should be spent.

A contractor is a person of many skills and talents who must orchestrate the many skills and talents of the subcontractors working on the project. He or she must be a master builder, troubleshooter, shrewd shopper, manager, and facilitator, and must be organized enough to get the job done in the shortest time within the specified budget. It is his or her job to direct the project from start to finish, including supervising any demolition and finding, hiring, and managing the subcontractors—the plumber, electrician, tile installer, painter, carpenter, and anyone involved in the construction. The contractor also orders materials, supervises the schedules of the subcontractors, applies for the building permit (also called the work permit), deals with the local bureaucracy, schedules inspector visits as needed, and manages the work crew on a daily basis.

The most important job your contractor performs is to handle all the minor and major daily problems that arise, coming up with viable solutions that keep the project progressing to meet your schedule.

A GLOSSARY OF BATHROOM TERMS

When redesigning, remodeling, or constructing a bathroom, you may encounter some words you do not recognize. Here are a few of them.

apron   the front vertical extension of the bathtub from the rim to the floor.

base cabinets   in the bathroom, the cabinets located under the countertop in a vanity.

built-in   a cabinet, shelf, or other storage unit positioned in a recessed manner so that it is flush with the surrounding wall.

enclosure   panels of glass or other material used to form a shower or tub stall.

fitting   the plumbing and associated devices that bring water to the fixtures. Fittings include showerheads, spouts, faucets, drains, diverter valves, and water supply lines.

fixture   something that is fixed or attached in a bathroom as a permanent structural part. Bathroom fixtures are the tub, shower, toilet, lavatory, and bidet.

lavatory or lav   a fixed bowl or basin for washing with running water and a drainpipe.

pedestal   a stand-alone lavatory whose basin and supporting column are one continuous piece.

pressure balance valve   a control device used in shower fixtures that prevents surges of extremely hot or cold water.

surround   the enclosure around a bathtub or whirlpool that includes areas surrounding the tub, such as platform and steps.

vanity   the support used to hold a drop-in bathroom sink, consisting of a countertop and an underneath cabinet usually used for storage. It also is a small dressing table.

whirlpool   a tub that utilizes water jets to massage the bather, and fills and drains like a standard tub.

A Bathroom for All

Designing your bathroom creates a variety of challenges and opportunities. Many people think about color, taste, trends, lifestyle, location in the home, and usage, but never consider this room's usefulness in the future.

Do not fall into the trap of designing only for the present. Granted, many people do not need a bathroom that is wheelchair accessible. However, we all grow old, or we may have to care for an elderly parent or a handicapped family member. It makes sense when redesigning your bathroom to incorporate the following objectives into your plan:

Floor space Even the tiniest bathrooms, if well designed, can accommodate your requirements. The key is careful planning and effective utilization of the space based on lifestyle, personal needs, and usage. Greater floor space allows an adult to wash and care for youngsters, an elderly parent to use a walker or cane easily in the bathroom, or a wheelchair-bound individual to maneuver to the toilet or shower.

Wider doorways and flush saddles (sills) Most accidents that occur in the home occur in the bathroom. Low saddles or saddles flush to the floor prevent trips and stubbed toes and make access easier for small children and people with limited mobility. Wider doorways provide easier circulation.

Grab bars Every bathroom should incorporate a grab bar in the tub and shower area. It will provide needed support for older bathers, young children, injured family members, the physically challenged, and anyone assisting with the care of others.

Adequate lighting Besides ambient or mood lighting, proper task lighting is an absolute must for the bathroom. If your lighting is too dim or insufficient for your family, change it.

Special fixtures for the handicapped Many manufacturers produce special shower stalls, tubs, toilets, sinks, and vanities for the physically challenged. If you have a family member who is wheelchair-bound or requires the assis-

A separate curved shower stall with an extra-long towel bar has a wooden slat floor in this art-filled bathroom designed by Lembo-Bohn.

tance of a walker, cane, or braces, install these fixtures; they can be used by all family members. A bathroom designed for the handicapped need not look institutional or ugly. These fixtures are available in many colors, styles, and finishes. Research and compare various manufacturers' offerings before making a decision.

Faucets, towel bars, and accessories Before purchasing anything for your bathroom, carefully consider who is going to use that space. If you have small children or elderly parents, for instance, delicate, ornate faucets are not the right choice. To avoid scalding, select larger-handled faucets that are easy to turn and clearly marked. Fixtures are available with colored markers for young children who cannot read or individuals with limited vision. Avoid toilet paper holders and towel bars with sharp edges and points. Select a spot on the wall that will make towels and tissue easy to reach for everyone in your household. Pay attention to details. Make certain scatter rugs are securely anchored to avoid trips, glass shelves are out of the reach of young hands, wastebaskets are placed in an obvious spot, and storage areas are accessible to all.

Store all medicines, razor blades, and bath products in a cabinet that can be child-proofed. Electrical outlets should be locked or child-proofed to avoid shock. Hair dryers should not be placed near sinks, toilets, or tubs. Fixture height should be addressed for a bathroom used predominantly by smaller children.

WHAT THE INITIALS MEAN

As you consider the services of various professionals, you will come across many acronyms:

ADA: American Disabilities Act. This law was passed by Congress to prevent inaccessibility to public spaces, transportation, and facilities for those with special needs. In order to create a standard for universal accessibility, certain guidelines were established. Today many bath products are required to follow these guidelines.

AIA: American Institute of Architects. This is the national professional organization for architects, with chapters across the country. For more information about architects in your area, write the national office at 1735 New York Avenue NW, Washington, DC 20006 for more information. Architects must be licensed to practice architecture, but they are not required to join the AIA.

ANSI: American National Standards Institute. This standards body sets the guidelines of product acceptability for safety, durability, and endurance.

CBD: Certified Bathroom Designer. This certification comes from the National Kitchen & Bath Association, which can provide a list of CBDs in your area. Contact the NKBA at 687 Willow Grove Street, Hackettstown, NJ 07840.

CGR: Certified Graduate Remodeler. The Remodelers' Council of the National Association of Home Builders will provide a list of CGR contractors in your area. Contact the NAHB at 15th and M Street NW, Washington, DC 20005.

CR: Certified Remodeler. For a list of CR contractors near you, send a self-addressed stamped envelope to the National Association of the Remodeling Industry, 1901 North Moore Street, Arlington, VA 22209.

Bathroom Planning Guidelines

The National Kitchen & Bath Association (NKBA) has been the leading organization dedicated exclusively to the kitchen and bathroom design industry for more than two decades. Members include manufacturers, designers, dealers, and other industry professionals. NKBA provides consumer educational publications, kitchen and bath designer certification programs, and a variety of other educational programs and member services. For more information on NKBA contact: National Kitchen & Bath Association, 687 Willow Grove Street, Hackettstown, NJ 07840. Telephone: 908-852-0033; fax: 908-852-1695.

The guidelines recommended for bathroom design by the NKBA can serve as a good starting point for your project. They include:

1. A clear walkway of at least 32 inches should be provided at all entrances to the bathroom.
2. No doors should interfere with fixtures.
3. A mechanical ventilation system should be included in the plan.
4. Ground-fault circuit interrupters should be specified on all receptacles. No switches should be placed within 60 inches of any water source. All light fixtures above tub/shower units should be moisture-proof fixtures.
5. If floor space exists between two fixtures, at least 6 inches of space should be provided for cleaning.
6. At least 21 inches of clear walkway space should exist in front of the lavatory.
7. The minimum recommended clearance from the lavatory centerline to any side wall is 12 inches.
8. The minimum recommended clearance between two bowls in the lavatory is 30 inches, centerline to centerline.
9. The minimum recommended clearance from the center of the toilet to any obstruction, fixture, or equipment on either side of the toilet is 15 inches.

Intricately carved marble covers the sink, basin, backsplash area and walls in this elegant bathroom from the twenties.

10. At least 21 inches of clear walkway space should exist in front of the toilet.

11. The toilet paper holder should be installed within reach of a person seated on the toilet. The ideal location is slightly in front of the edge of the toilet bowl, the center of which is 26 inches above the finished floor.

12. The minimum recommended clearance from the center of the bidet to any obstruction, fixture, or equipment on either side of the bidet is 15 inches.

13. At least 21 inches of clear walkway space should exist in front of the bidet.

14. Storage for soap and towels should be installed within reach of a person seated on the bidet.

15. No more than one step should lead to the tub. The step should be at least 10 inches deep, and should not exceed 7¼ inches in height.

16. Bathtub faucetry should be accessible from outside the tub.

17. Whirlpool motor access, if necessary, should be included in the plan.

18. At least one grab bar should be installed to facilitate bathtub or shower entry.

19. The minimum recommended usable shower interior dimension is 32 inches by 32 inches.

20. A bench or footrest should be installed within the shower enclosure.

21. A minimum clear walkway of 21 inches should exist in front of the tub/shower.

22. The shower door should swing into the bathroom.

23. All showerheads should be protected by pressure balance/temperature regulators or by temperature-limiting devices.

24. All flooring should be of slip-resistant material.

25. Adequate storage should be provided in the plan, including: counter/shelf space around the lavatory, adequate grooming equipment storage, convenient shampoo and soap storage in the shower/tub area, and hanging space for bathroom linens.

26. An adequate heating system should be provided.

27. General and task lighting should be provided.

A mirror set into the wall is covered with a tromp l'oeil "curtain" in this small guest bath under the eaves in a Bucks County farmhouse. Designer Jeffrey Bilhuber had the moldings painted a faux bamboo, which emphasizes the room's irregular shape.

Visual
Resources

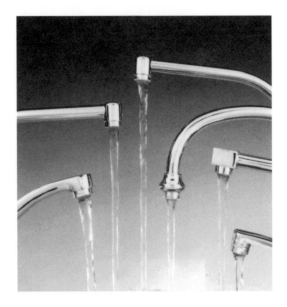

Sinks
Faucets
Tubs
Showers/Enclosures
Toilets
Cabinets
Tiles
Lighting
Accessories
Products for the Physically Challenged

Sinks

1. The nautically inspired America's Cup ensemble from Hastings Tile & Il Bagno is a chrome-plated brass pedestal with a mirror-polished stainless-steel basin designed to use minimal space.

2. Available in 28-inch and 29-inch versions and as a duo (two bowls on a single pedestal base), the Harmonia series of vitreous china pedestal basins is by Kallista.

3. The Dino pattern has been hand-painted onto the heritage pedestal lav by American China.

4. The Monte Carlo II basin from Kallista is available in oval, round, and octagonal shapes and features a highly polished rim that contrasts with the hammered bowl interior.

5. Avonite's Blue Monolith vanity is hand-chiseled and shown with brass fixtures.

6. The Revival pedestal lavatory by Kohler contains an oval basin with a wide, sweeping rim. The pedestal comes with either a tapered base that flares upward to the basin or scrolled lever handles resting on a round doric column.

7. The Ceres sink from Avonite, with a bowl interior measuring 13¾ inches by 9¾ inches, is designed specifically for small spaces.

8. Barclay's Duckies has a self-rim, drop-in lavatory bowl.

9. Composed of durable fire-clay ceramic, this 36-inch Belle Epoque console from Barclay features sculpted vitreous china legs.

10. The console table from Kohler's Revival collection features an oval basin with a generously proportioned rim and slender metal legs available in either chrome or brass.

11. The Floral Chinoiserie bowl design by Sherle Wagner combines floral patterns rimmed in 24-karat gold with coordinated base fittings.

1

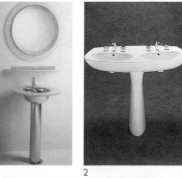

2

3

4

5

6

7

8

9

10

11

Faucets

1. The Girotondo collection of faucets and fittings from Hastings Tile & Il Bagno is available in chrome or gold finishes, and features knobs and rings as design elements.

2. The widespread lavatory set named Lawrence from Chicago Faucet is shown featuring a metal cross handle faucet.

3. The Moen Monticello lavatory faucet comes in a polished brass finish with Glacier lever handle inserts.

4. The Sophisticate faucet from Chicago Faucet features tiered rounded edges on both handle blades and spout.

5. The Water Rainbow bath spout by Jacuzzi is available in chrome or brass metallic finishes, with rope, ring, or bank handle accents.

6. Shown here is a montage of Moen deluxe and adjustable spray showerheads.

7. The Jetline faucet from Jado features forward-angled knobs or lever handles and a dynamic spout in either polished chrome or silver nickel/gold.

8. The 2001 faucet series from Jado is available as a single-lever lavatory set.

9. The Athos faucet by Kallista comes in five finishes and offers wooden sleeves, as well as the option of custom-colored metal sleeves to match any bathroom decor.

10. The Swan basin set by Sherle Wagner features 24-karat gold plate.

11. A diverter spout and a mechanism that controls constant hot and cold water temperatures are included with the Argenti pressure tub and shower set by Barclay.

12. Grohe's ¾-inch thermostat valve is pictured here.

13. Single-handle control is the prominent feature of Kohler's Paladar lavatory faucets with cast brass bodies and ceramic.

1

2

3

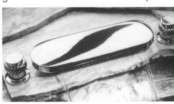

4

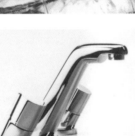

5

6

7

8

9

10

11

12

13

Tubs

1. The hand-carved Rose Aurora marble tub with malachite tiles is from Sherle Wagner.

2. Porcher's Ardennes is a sculptured cast-iron tub that fits into a space 60 inches by 30 inches, but is a deeper $16\frac{1}{2}$ inches for more comfortable adult bathing.

3. The Revival 6-foot whirlpool from Kohler is designed with an integral faucet deck, lumbar supports, and a 20-minute safety shutdown mechanism.

4. The two-person acrylic Sojourn whirlpool from Kohler is styled with a basin tucked inside a five-sided neo-angle for corner installation.

5. The streamlined Aspen whirlpool by Swirlway features a contoured backrest and adjustable jets to provide various types of hydromassage.

6. Designed for two, the Fontana whirlpool from Jacuzzi features water cascading down a central stair step and a European-style hand-held shower.

7. Crafted of reinforced fiberglass, the half-moon-shaped Maurea whirlpool is a two-person tub with adjustable jets and a seat for bathside grooming.

8. The Cortina whirlpool bath by Jacuzzi is made of high-gloss acrylic reinforced with fiberglass and features four adjustable jets, a contoured back support, and an integral seat for bathside grooming.

9. The Sabella whirlpool from Jacuzzi features four fully adjustable Power Pro jets coupled with four directionally adjustable neck jets.

10. An elliptical rim that encloses a slightly off-center elliptical bathing basin characterizes the 6-foot Seaside whirlpool from Kohler.

11. Measuring 72 inches long by 60 inches wide, the Alexa from Jacuzzi offers a compact spa with seven jets.

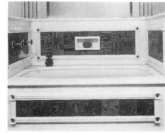

1

2

3

4

5

6

7

8

9

10

11

Showers/ Enclosures

1. The Regency Frameless Enclosure by Majestic Shower Company features tempered safety glass panels fixed permanently to the shower pan and walls.

2. This glass bathscreen by Majestic Shower Company, available in several color options, is composed of a single sheet of smooth, tempered safety-glass that swings open on polished hinges for easy tub access.

3. Kohler's Sonata shower module includes a Mastershower tower and an angled-corner shape constructed of acrylic for easy care.

4. The J-Carré shower system from Jacuzzi incorporates an eight-function shower nozzle and sixteen programmable jets along with a sculpted seat and built-in cabinet and shelves.

5. Jacuzzi whirlpool's J-Shower features a full-size whirlpool bath with four jets combined with a curved shower enclosure.

6. The J-Dream II shower system from Jacuzzi offers each user a personal set of sixteen hydrotherapy jets, a sculpted seat, and water cascades, as well as adjustable hand-held showers with eight massage settings.

7. The Crystal Daylite shower enclosure by American Shower Door boasts solid brass hinges and accessories with invisible, leakproof panels.

1

2

3

4

5

6

7

Toilets

1. The new Portrait toilet by Kohler, with matching pedestal lavatory, is shown with an Epernay design pattern reminiscent of hand-painted 18th-century French earthenware.

2. The beauty of the marbelized finish plus the durability of solid plastic is shown in this sculpted toilet cover by Sanderson that overlaps the scalloped seat ring.

3. This marbelized, high-gloss-finish toilet seat from Sanderson can be lifted off the toilet bowl for thorough cleaning without removing the hinges.

4. Porcher's Calla Collection includes 24-inch and 28-inch pedestal lavatories, a self-rimming toilet, and a bidet.

5. This high-tank toilet is from the Victoria line by Barclay.

6. Hand-painted details, including a monogram, adorn the Bisbee one-piece toilet, the Sedona drop-in lavatory, and the Lagua bidet, all by American China.

7. The White Coquille suite of fixtures by Porcher includes bidet, toilet, and pedestal lavatory.

8. The ripple design of this toilet seat by Sanderson offers an art deco style and is molded of wood composition.

9. The Revival Lite toilet by Kohler has a rounded base and oval tank lid, and features a water-saving 1.6-gallon flush and a pull-knob flush actuator on the top of the tank.

10. The Revival bidet by Kohler features a unique, through-the-rim horizontal spray that reduces splashing, and a three-hole punching that can accommodate widespread faucet sprays.

1

2

3

4

5

6

7

8

9

10

Cabinets

1. PL Bath Products' Premier line medicine cabinet system is shown as four cabinets and lights assembled to create a four-door unit.

2. The M Series 30-inch cabinet by Robern features a glass medicine chest stacking system, shown here with a sink module.

3. The cabinet module stacking system by Robern is completely mirrored inside and out, and comes with swing-out doors and high-quality glass shelving.

4. The M Series by Robern, featuring 6-inch-deep cabinets with flexible glass shelving, provides twice as much storage space as a standard medicine cabinet.

5. Robern's F Series cabinets are constructed of colored anodized aluminum framed doors with a choice of four different door glasses in place of the standard mirror.

6. Rev-a-Shelf's Hide-a-Step is a concealed, easily installed fold-out step platform that mounts flat against the inside of bathroom cabinet doors and can support up to 200 pounds.

7. Allowing three-way viewing when the 16-inch doors are fully open, Robern's C Series two-door cabinets come with theatrical top lighting.

8. This cabinet stacking system by Robern features a two-stacked cabinet module with a central mirrored medicine chest and includes a vertical, tubular, dual-incandescent light source.

9. The Wellcroft custom cabinetry by Wellborn is shown with a circular vanity, flanked by a glass cabinet over drawer built-ins.

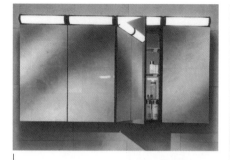

1

2

3

4

5

6

7

8

9

Tiles

1. The Floral Collection from Italian Ceramic Tile includes florals designed with a touch of tradition, available in contemporary palettes.

2. Various tiles for floor, wall, and decorative usage are from Laufen International.

3. Fornasetti Bohemian Glasses from Hastings Tile & Il Bagno are available in 8-inch-by-8-inch tiles as a set of eight different designs.

4. Floor tiles from Italian Ceramic Tile include mosaics, stonelike designs, terra-cotta, and rustic looks in a broad range of tones.

5.–7. Ranging from hand-crafted mosaics to animal figures, these tiles by Ann Sacks, a Kohler Company, are available in many colors, materials, and finishes.

8. Laufen International's Medici Royale is shown here in wall and complementary decorative tile.

9. Various patterns and colors from Armstrong's Visions Solarian and Solarian II collections complement almost any bath decor.

10. Soli e Lune ceramic wall tiles from Hastings Tile & Il Bagno are silk-screened with twelve different graphic black-and-white sun and moon images.

1

2

3

4

5

6

7

8

9

10

Lighting

1. Lightolier's Bath Lighting by Forecast includes deco fluorescent bath strips with a white translucent bullnose acrylic diffuser and polished brass inserts capped by cast art deco ends.

2. The Dual Source Light by Robern combines incandescent and fluorescent bulbs that can be lit individually or simultaneously, allowing the user to control the light intensity and to match the light color to specific environmental needs.

3. Frosted glass bowls that provide pure white light directed upward for general-purpose illumination are a feature of Lightolier's Bath Lighting by Forecast.

4. Quad, part of the LC230 Series from Capri Lighting, is an adjustable accent light with a stepped pyramidal trim that frames an adjustable bezel; it accepts a variety of low-voltage lamps.

5. The DL-1000-30 High Intensity Bar Light by NuTone features a beveled-edge, arched toplight with decorative maple wood panel overlay; it provides high-intensity downlighting from four tungsten halogen bulbs.

6. Lightolier's Bath Lighting by Forecast line includes elongated octagonal mirrored backplate fixtures as an alternative to the common theatrical strip.

7. A generous ceiling height and spacious wall surface accommodate a pendant fixture complete with alabaster bowl and flanking twin uplight sconces by Lightolier.

8. A shatter-resistant acrylic enclosure with a single-ended compact fluorescent tube constitutes Helios by Lightolier, a light fixture that offers high energy efficiency, long life, and good color rendering.

9. The Showerlite Drop Opal Lens (71PS) by Halo Lighting is designed specifically for use in damp locations.

1

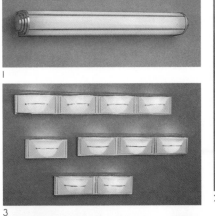

2

3

7

4

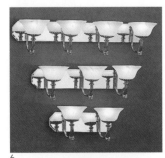

6

5

8

9

Accessories

1. Waterware Inc.'s Winflatables are inflatable pillows for use in the bath.

2. The Summer Country Seabrook wallcovering from Thompson & Company is shown with matching shower curtain, sink skirt, window shade, and bathroom furniture upholstery.

3. Blome's Etrusca collection of accessories features Xolon holdbacks and Volterra, Chiusi, and Orvieto rods, all in rust.

4. NuTone's Ambassador series of bathroom accessories comes in polished chrome and features concealed screw mountings. The detail photograph shows the soap dish.

5. Traditionally styled solid brass accessories from Baldwin's Chesapeake line include a robe hook, a towel bar, and a towel ring.

6. Easy-to-clean glass shelves from Barclay's Victoria line come in a choice of finishes, including gold, brass, chrome-plated, or a combination of chrome and brass trim.

7. The Gap is one of the many upscale stores that, in response to the tremendous surge in consumer interest in the bathroom, now offer a full range of stylish bath products.

8. The EB Series of Myson Towel Warmers is a self-contained unit available in chrome, brass, or gold plate.

9. The UltraValve Intelligent Bathing System by Memry Corporation is an easy-to-install electronics water temperature control that accurately and safely monitors water temperature in the shower or bath. The UltraValve turns water on or off, includes protection against scalding, and shows the selected temperature in an easy-to-read LED display.

10. The Epoca from Hastings Tile & Il Bagno is a beveled-edge mirror framed in flowing glass that encircles it in a broad, ribbonlike band.

1

2

3

4

5

6

7

9

8

10

Products for the Physically Challenged

1

2

1. E. L. Mustee & Son's new barrier-free #360 Durabase shower floor and entry ramp is designed in compliance with ADA specifications, and features a molded fiberglass 30-inch-by-60-inch floor and a 12-inch-by-60-inch entry ramp. The two-piece design can be used in new construction or to replace a standard 5-foot bathtub, utilizing the existing drain hookup.

2. The Precedence bath whirlpool from Kohler is equipped with a door that swings inward for easy access to the bath; the HydroLoc door seal inflates automatically when the bath begins to fill with water.

3. Featuring a removable transfer seat so that bathers can sit down and swing their legs over the edge of the tub, instead of stepping into it, the Freewill bath/shower module from Kohler is crafted of durable, glossy acrylic and is available in many colors.

4. This wheelchair-accessible shower is from Kohler's Freewill line of barrier-free bathing units; the first in the industry to be designed for compatibility with residential settings, the line also meets institutional requirements for durability and easy maintenance.

5. Equipped with side grip rails and crafted with a slip-resistant Safeguard bottom, the Guardian bath by Kohler is designed for safe entrance and exit. Styled with a beveled edge and measuring 60 by 32 by 16¼ inches, the enameled cast-iron bath is designed to fit the standard bathtub alcove and is available in a wide range of colors.

6. This compact barrier-free shower module is part of Kohler's Freewill line. Available in six different colors, the unit features a fold-up seat.

3

4

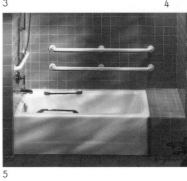

5

6

Directory

Architects & Designers

Agrest and Gandelsonas
740 Broadway, 10th Floor
New York, NY 10003
212-260-9100

Architects Santa Fe
343 Manhattan Avenue
Santa Fe, NM 87501
505-983-4078
•
Bilhuber, Inc.
330 East 59th Street
New York, NY 10022
212-308-4888

Karin Blake
49A Malibu Colony
Malibu, CA 90265
310-456-8010

' L. Bogdanow & Associates
75 Spring Street
New York, NY 10012
212-966-0313

Agnes Bourne
2 Henry Adams Street, #220
San Francisco, CA 94103
415-626-6883

Brayton & Hughes, Design Studio
250 Sutter Street, Suite 650
San Francisco, CA 94108
415-291-8100

Bromley Caldari Architects
242 West 27th Street
New York, NY 10001
212-620-4250
•
Michael de Santis
1110 Second Avenue, #203
New York, NY 10022
212-753-8871

Drysdale Design Associates, Inc.
1733 Connecticut Avenue NW
Washington, DC 20009
202-588-0700

•
1100 Architect
435 Hudson Street, 8th Floor
New York, NY 10014
212-645-1011
•
Robert Federighi
Federighi Food Machinery Inc.
70 13th Street
San Francisco, CA 94103
415-626-2800

Francis Fleetwood Architects
25 Newtown Lane
East Hampton, NY 11937
516-324-4994
•
Glenn Gissler Design
174 Fifth Avenue, #204
New York, NY 10010
212-727-3220
•
Victoria Hagan Interiors
22 East 72nd Street
New York, NY 10021
212-472-1290
•
Kitty Hawks
136 East 57th Street
New York, NY 10021
212-832-3810

Benjamin Huntington
271 Fifth Avenue
New York, NY 10016
212-213-9698

Gary Hutton Design
2100 Bryant Street
San Francisco, CA 94110
415-282-4787
•
Johnson & Wanzenberg
211 West 61st Street
New York, NY 10023
212-489-7840
•
Paul Krause Architect
16 The Parkway
Katonah, NY 10536
914-232-8104
•
McBride & Associates
560 Broadway
New York, NY 10012
212-941-0818

Jessica McClintock
1400 16th Street
San Francisco, CA 94103
415-495-3030

Andrea and Marc Michaelson
1196 Summit Drive
Beverly Hills, CA 90210
310-271-7911

J. P. Molyneux Studio Ltd.
29 East 69th Street
New York, NY 10021
212-628-0097

Charles Morris Mount Inc.
300 West 108th Street
New York, NY 10025
212-864-2937
•
Passanella & Klein, Stolzman & Berg
330 West 42nd Street
New York, NY 10036
212-594-2010

Barbara Scavullo Design
251 Rhode Island Street, Suite 105
San Francisco, CA 94103
415-558-8774

Leslie Horan Simon
Horan, Inc.
55 Central Park West
New York, NY 10023
212-873-1373

Siskin-Valls, Inc.
21 West 58th Street
New York, NY 10019
212-752-3790

Stephanie Stokes Inc.
790 Madison Avenue
New York, NY 10021
212-744-3379

Max Wolfe Sturman Architects
3300 Rice Street, Suite 11
Coconut Grove, FL 33133
305-441-1171
•
Michael Trapp
7 River Road
West Cornwall, CT 06796
203-672-6098
•
Vicente Wolf Associates, Inc.
333 West 39th Street
New York, NY 10018
212-465-0590

Manufacturers

Aamsco Manufacturing, Inc.
P.O. Box 15119
Jersey City, NJ 07305
201-434-0722

Allmilmo Corp.
P.O. Box 629, 70 Clinton Road
Fairfield, NJ 07004-2976 .
201-227-2502

American Olean Tile Co.
100 Cannon Avenue
Lansdale, PA 19446
215-855-1111

American Shower Door
P.O. Box 30010
Los Angeles, CA 90030
800-421-2333

American Standard, Inc.
1 Centennial Plaza
P.O. Box 6820
Piscataway, NJ 08855
201-980-3000

Americh Corp.
13208 Faticoy Street
N. Hollywood, CA 91605
800-453-1463

Ann Sacks Tile & Stone
500 N.W. 23rd Avenue
Portland, OR 97210
800-488-TILE (West Coast)
800-377-TILE (East Coast)

Armstrong World Industries
P.O. Box 3001
Lancaster, PA 17604
800-233-3823

Artemide Lighting
1980 New Highway
Farmingdale, NY 11735
516-694-9292

Artistic Brass
4100 Ardmore Avenue
South Gate, CA 90280
800-877-4100

Avonite
5100 Goldleaf Parkway
Suite 200
Los Angeles, CA 90056
800-4-AVONITE

•
Baldwin Hardware Corporation
841 East Wyomissing Boulevard
P.O. Box 15048
Reading, PA 19612
215-777-7811

Barclay Products
4000 Porrett Drive
Gurnee, IL 60031-1246
708-244-1234

Bates
3699 Industry Avenue
Lakewood, CA 90712
310-595-8824

Bemis Manufacturing Company
Sheboygan Falls, WI 53085
414-467-4621

Blome
74 Henry Street
Secaucus, NJ 07094
800-875-0042

Bobrick Corporation
60 East 42nd Street
New York, NY 10017
212-867-6969

Broadway Industries
The Broadway Collection
250 N. Troost
Olathe, KS 66061
800-766-1661

BTC Inc.
Route 6, Box 560-G
New Braunfels, TX 78132
210-629-5887
•
The Chicago Faucet Co.
2100 S. Nuclear Drive
Des Plaines, IL 60018
708-803-5000

Color Tile
515 Houston Street
Fort Worth, TX 77210
713-739-5400

Cooper Lighting
P.O. Box 4446
Houston, TX 77210
713-739-5400

Corian Products
DuPont Co.
PPD Dept.
Wilmington, DE 19898
800-4-CORIAN

Creative Visions in Marketing
312-467-1177

CR Specialties
6120 Grand Central Parkway
Forest Hills, NY 11375
718-268-9538

Czech & Speake available at:
    Mary Corley
    1425 Dragon Street
    Dallas, TX 75207
    214-744-4947

    Eurobath & Tile
    Stonemill Design Centre
    2915 Redhill Avenue, Suite 102
    Costa Mesa, CA 92626
    714-545-2284

    Howard Kaplan Antiques
    827 Broadway
    New York, NY 10003
    212-674-1000

    Royal Appointments, Ltd.
    443 N. Clark Street
    Chicago, IL 60610
    312-222-9666

    Waterworks
    29 Park Avenue
    Danbury, CT 06810
    203-792-9979
•
D. Porthault & Co.
18 East 69th Street
New York, NY 10021
212-688-1661

Dacor
950 S. Raymond Avenue
Pasadena, CA 91109
818-799-1000

Dornbracht
1202 West Loop North
Houston, TX 77055
713-688-1862
•
E. L. Mustee & Sons, Inc.
5431 W. 164th Street
Cleveland, OH 44142
216-267-3100

Eljer Industries
901 10th Street
Plano, TX 75074
800-PL-ELJER
•
Florida Tile
A Division of Premark
P.O. Box 447
Lakeland, FL 33802
800-352-8453

Formica Corporation
10155 Reading Road
Cincinnati, OH 45241
513-786-3533

Franciscan Woodworks
24 Galli Drive
Novato, CA 94949
415-382-8281

Franke Inc.
212 Church Road
North Wales, PA 19454
215-699-8761

The French Reflection, Inc.
820 S. Robertson Boulevard
Los Angeles, CA 90035
310-659-3800

Frombruche
Classic Design
132 N. Main Street
Spring Valley, NY 10977
800-537-6319
•

George Kovacs Lighting, Inc.
67-25 Otto Road
Glendale, NY 11385
718-392-8190

Gerber Plumbing Fixtures Corp.
4656 W. Touhy Avenue
Chicago, IL 60646
708-675-6570

Groen
1900 Pratt Boulevard
Elk Grove Village, IL 60007
708-439-2400

Grohe America
241 Covington Drive
Bloomingdale, IL 60108
708-582-7711
•

Halo Lighting
6 West 20th Street
New York, NY 10011
212-645-4580

Harrington Brass Works
166 Coolidge Avenue
Englewood, NJ 07631
201-871-6011

Hastings Tile
Il Bagno Collection
30 Commercial Street
Freeport, NY 11520
516-379-3500

Hastings Tile
230 Park Avenue South
New York, NY 10003
212-674-9700

Hunter Douglas Inc.
2 Parkway, Route 17 S.
Upper Saddle River, NJ 07458
201-327-8200
•

Italian Tile Center
Division of Italian Trade
Commission
499 Park Avenue
New York, NY 10022
212-980-1500
•

Jacuzzi Inc.
2121 N. California Boulevard
Suite 475
Walnut Creek, CA 94596
510-938-7070

Jado Bath & Hardware Mfg. Co.
P.O. Box 1329
1690 Calle Quetzal
Camarillo, CA 93011
•

Kallista, Inc.
2701 Merced Street
San Leandro, CA 94577
510-895-6400

Kohler Co.
Kohler, WI 53044
414-457-1271

Kraft
306 East 61st Street
New York, NY 10021
212-838-2214

Kroin Hardware
180 Fawcett Street
Cambridge, MA 02138
617-492-4000
•

Laufen International
P.O. Box 6600
Tulsa, OK 74156
918-428-3851

Lightolier Inc.
100 Lighting Way
Secaucus, NJ 07096
201-864-3000
•

Majestic Shower Company
1795 Yosemite Avenue
San Francisco, CA 94124
415-822-1511

Memry Corporation
57 Commerce Drive
Brookfield, CT 06804
203-740-7311

Moen
377 Woodland Avenue
Elyria, OH 44036
216-323-3341

Monarch Tile
P.O. Box 999
Florence, AL 35631
205-764-6181

Myson Towel Warmers
20 Lincoln Street
Essex Junction, VT 05452
802-879-1170
•

Nevamar Corporation
8339 Telegraph Road
Odenton, MD 21113
301-551-5000

NuTone
Madison & Red Bank Roads
Cincinnati, OH 45227
800-543-8687
•

Outwater Plastics Industries
4 Passaic Street
Wood Ridge, NJ 07075
800-888-0880
•

Phylrich International
1000 N. Orange Drive
Los Angeles, CA 90038
800-421-3190

PL Bath Products
P.O. Box 262
Bensalem, PA 19020
800-488-2284

Porcher/American China
1516 Bradley Court
Naperville, IL 60565
708-961-2071
•

Rev-A-Shelf
2409 Plantside Drive
Jeffersontown, KY 40299
800-626-11126

Robern
1648 Winchester Road
Bensalem, PA 19020
800-877-2376

Runtal North America, Inc.
187 Neck Road
P.O. Box 8278
Ward Hill, MA 01835
800-526-2621
•

Sherle Wagner International Inc.
60 East 57th Street
New York, NY 10022
212-758-3300

Sign of the Crab, Ltd.
3756 Omec Circle
Rancho Cordova, CA 95742
916-638-2722

Simons Hardware & Bath
421 Third Avenue
New York, NY 10016
212-532-9220

Sussman-Automatic Corporation
(Mr. Steam and Warmatowel)
43-20 34th Street
Long Island City, NY 11101
800-767-8326

Swirl-Way Plumbing Group
P.O. Box 210
Henderson, TX 75653
800-999-1459
•

TFI Corporation
2812 Hegan Lane
Chico, CA 95928
916-891-6390

Thomas Lighting Group/Capri
Lighting
6430 E. Slauson Avenue
Los Angeles, CA 90040
213-726-1800

Thompson & Co.
65 Union Avenue, 8th Floor
Memphis, TN 38103
901-527-8000

The Ton Jon Company
56 S. LaSalle Street
Aurora, IL 60507
708-892-9208
•

Vermont Marble Co.
61 Main Street
Proctor, VT 05765
800-451-4468
•

Waterware, Inc.
15 West 81st Street
New York, NY 10024
212-874-1900

Wenczel Tile Co.
200 Enterprise Avenue
Trenton, NJ 08638
609-599-4503

Wilsonart
Ralph Wilson Plastics Co.
600 General Bruce Drive
Temple, TX 76501
800-433-3222
•

Zoeller Pump Co.
P.O. Box 16347
Louisville, KY 40256
800-928-PUMP

Suppliers

RETAIL OUTLETS,
CATALOGS, CRAFTSPEOPLE,
AND MORE

A & F NY
22 W. 21st Street
New York, NY 10010
800-366-2284

ABC Carpet & Home
888 Broadway
New York, NY 10003
212-473-3000

adaptAbility Catalog
P.O. Box 515
Colchester, CT 06415-0515
800-243-9232

AD HOC
410 W. Broadway
New York, NY 10012
212-925-2652

AliMed, Inc.
297 High Street
Dedham, MA 02026
800-248-2011

Ann Morris Antiques
239 E. 60th Street
New York, NY 10021
212-755-3308

Architectural Details
641 Country Road, 39A
Southampton, NY 11968

Architectural Lighting
1933 South Broadway, 1204
Los Angeles, CA 90007
213-742-8800

Attitudes Catalogue
1213 Elko Drive
Sunnyvale, CA 94089
800-525-2468
•

Ballard Designs Catalogue
1670 DeFoor Avenue NW
Atlanta, GA 30318
404-351-5099

The Bath and Beyond
135 Mississippi Street
San Francisco, CA 94103
415-552-5001

Bed Bath and Beyond
620 Avenue of the Americas
New York, NY 10011
212-255-3550

Bering Home Center
6102 Westheimer
Houston, TX 77057
713-785-6400

Brown & Jenkins Trading Co.
Catalog
Box 1570
Burlington, VT 05402
800-456-5282
•

Casella Lighting
111 Rhode Island Street
San Francisco, CA 94103
415-626-9600

Chamber's Catalog
P.O. Box 7841
San Francisco, CA 94120
800-334-9790

Christine Belfor, Ltd.
304 Hudson Street, Studio 600
New York, NY 10013
212-633-6680

Clarence House
211 East 58th Street
New York, NY 10022
212-752-2890

Classic Design
132 N. Main Street
Spring Valley, NY 10977
800-537-6319

Crate and Barrel Catalogue
P.O. Box 9059
Wheeling, IL 60090
800-323-5461

Creative Care
800-797-2029

Custom Accessories
4211 Richmond Avenue
Houston, TX 77027
713-961-1324
•

David Forster & Co.
750 Madison Avenue, 2nd Floor
New York, NY 10021
212-861-8989

Davis & Warshow, Inc.
P.O. Box 39
Maspeth, NY 11378
800-479-9504

Design Warehouse
1116 Corey Avenue
Los Angeles, CA 90069
310-858-1878

Design With Lighting
1140 Folsom Street
San Francisco, CA 94103
800-229-2410

Domaine
661-120th NE
Bellevue, WA 98006
206-450-9900

•
Endurance Floor Co.
18460 N.E. Second Avenue
Miami, FL 33179
305-652-6481

Enrichments for Better Living
Catalog
145 Tower Drive
P.O. Box 579
Hinsdale, IL 60521
800-323-5547

Eurobath
7700 N. Trail
Naples, FL 33963
813-597-8118

Evergreen House
4545 N. Charles Street
Baltimore, MD 21210
410-516-0341

•
F & M Plumbing Supply
631 East 9th Street
New York, NY 10009
800-834-0990

Fishs Eddy
889 Broadway
New York, NY 10003
212-420-9020

Fortune's Almanac
150 Chestnut Street
San Francisco, CA 94111-1004
800-331-2300

•
The Gap, Inc.
1 Harrison Street
San Francisco, CA 94105
415-952-4400

Garnet Hill
262 Main Street
Franconia, NH 03580
800-622-6216

Guess Home Collection
465 W. Broadway
New York, NY 10012
212-982-9055

•
Hold Everything Catalog
P.O. Box 7807
San Francisco, CA 94120-7807
800-541-2233

The Home Depot
2727 Paces Ferry Road
Atlanta, GA 30339
404-433-8211

Home Town
131 Wooster Street
New York, NY 10012
212-674-5770

Home Trends Catalog
779 Mt. Read Boulevard
Rochester, NY 14606
716-254-6520

The Horchow Home Collection
P.O. Box 620048
Dallas, TX 75262-0048
800-456-7000

Zoltan Horvath
500 Piermont Avenue
Hillsdale, NJ 07642
201-666-6688

Howard Kaplan's Bath Shop
47 E. 12th Street
New York, NY 10003
212-674-1000

H$_2$O Plus
845 W. Madison Avenue
Chicago, IL 60607-2631
800-242-2284

Christopher Hyland, Inc.
979 Third Avenue
New York, NY 10022
212-688-6121

•
Ikea US Inc.
Plymouth Commons
Plymouth Meeting, PA 19462
412-747-0747

Independent Living Aids, Inc.,
Catalog
27 East Mall
Plainview, NY 11803
800-537-2118

Indigo Seas
123 N. Robertson Boulevard
Los Angeles, CA 90048
310-550-8758

International Kitchen Bed & Bath
191 South Rand Road
Lake Zurich, IL 60047
708-540-6067

•
Jerome Sutter, Inc.
1167 Second Avenue
New York, NY 10017
212-688-7838

John Rosselli Ltd.
255 E. 72nd Street
New York, NY 10021
212-737-2252

•
KALA
5 Division Street
East Greenwich, RI 02818
401-885-1291

Kitchen & Bath Sourcebook (annual)
MBC Data Distribution Publications
3901 W. 86th Street, Suite 330
Indianapolis, IN 46268
317-875-7776

Klaff's
28 Washington Street
South Norwalk, CT 06854
203-866-1603

•
La France
550 15th Street
San Francisco, CA 94103
415-861-2977

LaNatura
425 N. Bedford Drive
Beverly Hills, CA 90210
310-271-5616

Lands' End Direct Merchants
Lands' End Inc.
1 Lands' End Lane
Dodgeville, WI 53595
800-356-4444

Laurel Designs
5 Laurel Avenue
Belvedere, CA 94920
415-435-1891

Laytner's Linen & Home
2270 Broadway
New York, NY 10024
212-724-0180

L'Herbier de Provence, Ltd.
100 Greyrock Place
Stamford, CT 06901
203-324-7922

Lillian Vernon Catalog
Virginia Beach, VA 23479-0002
804-430-1500

Lumex
100 Spence Street
Bay Shore, NY 11706
800-645-5272

Lynnens
278 Greenwich Avenue
Greenwich, CT 06830
203-629-3659
•

Macy's The Cellar
151 West 34th Street
New York, NY 10001
212-695-4400

Maddak, Inc.
6 Industrial Road
Pequannok, NJ 07440
201-628-7600

Markline Catalogue
P.O. Box 8
Elmira, NY 14902
800-225-8390

Martine Lionel-Dupont
Mosaic Tile Designs
Le Champ des Biens
78630 Orgeval, France
011-331-39-75-75-00

Modern Classics Gifts
22 Purchase Street
Rye, NY 10580
914-921-1484

Museum Collections Catalogue
921 Eastwind Drive
Westerville, OH 43081-3341
800-442-2460
•

Origins
100 Greyrock Place
Stamford, CT 06901
800-723-7310

Osborne & Little
979 Third Ave, 520
New York, NY 10022
212-751-3333
•

Patterson, Flynn & Martin
979 Third Avenue
New York, NY 10022
212-688-7700

Pero Group, Inc.
34 Wildwood Road
New Rochelle, NY 10804
914-834-1182

Portico
379 W. Broadway
New York, NY 10012
212-941-7800

Pottery Barn
P.O. Box 7044
San Francisco, CA 94120-7044
800-922-5507

Preferred Living
Clermont County Airport
Batavia, OH 45103
800-543-8633
•

Ralph Lauren Home Collection
867 Madison Avenue
New York, NY 10026
212-606-2100

Real Goods Trading Corp.
Catalogue
966 Mazzoni Street
Ukiah, CA 95482
800-762-7325

Resolute
1013 Stewart Street
Seattle, WA 98101
206-343-9323
•

The Safety Zone Catalog
Hanover, PA 17333-0019
800-999-3030

Sears, Roebuck & Co.
Sears Tower
Chicago, IL 60684
800-741-2568

Self-Care Catalog
580 Shellmound Street
Emeryville, CA 94662-0813
800-345-3371

Sentimento
306 East 61st Street
New York, NY 10021
212-750-3111

Shelly Tile
979 Third Avenue
New York, NY 10022
212-832-2255

Paul Smith
108 Fifth Avenue
New York, NY 10011
212-627-9770

Smith & Hawken
2 Arbor Lane, Box 6900
Florence, KY 41022
800-776-3336

Solutions Catalog
P.O. Box 6878
Portland, OR 97228
800-342-9988

Studio Bath & Tile
A Division of N&S Supply, Inc.
Old Route 6
Brewster, NY 10509
914-278-4702

Susquehanna Rehab Products
RD 2, Box 1
Wrightsville, PA 17368
800-248-2011
•

Ten Thousand Waves
P.O. Box 10103
Santa Fe, NM 87504
505-982-9304

Terracotta
11922 San Vicente
Los Angeles, CA 90049
310-826-7878

Terra Verde
120 Wooster Street
New York, NY 10012
212-925-4533

Tilecraft Ltd.
438 W. Francisco Boulevard
San Rafael, CA 94901
415-456-0282

Treillage Ltd.
418 E. 75th Street
New York, NY 10021
212-535-2288

Twin Farms
Stage Road
Barnard, VT 05031
800-894-6327
•

Urban Archaeology Co.
285 Lafayette Street
New York, NY 10012
212-431-6969
•

Vermont Country Store Catalog
P.O. Box 3000
Manchester Center, VT 05255
802-362-2400

Waterworks
Bathroom & Tiles
79 East Putnam Avenue
Greenwich, CT 06830
203-869-7766

Westchester Marble & Granite
610 S. Fulton Avenue
Mt. Vernon, NY 10550
800-634-0866

Winterthur Museum and Gardens
Catalogue
Dover, DE 19901
800-767-0500

Wolfman–Gold & Good Company
116 Greene Street
New York, NY 10012
212-431-1888

Acknowledgments

As always, a special thanks to my husband, Kevin, who contributed in many, many ways to this book, and to my sons, Patrick and Nicky, for their love, patience, and understanding during this journey, and to my extended family, especially the "Seven Sisters." I am also indebted to my incredible support team of Andrew Gentile, Sam Schwartz, Andy Lask, and David Lawrence, who helped me keep body and soul together.

I am especially grateful to John Vaughan, an extraordinary photographer, who will be missed. Many thanks to the brilliant work and generosity of Tim Street-Porter, Jennifer Levy, Rick Albert, and Steve Pierson, whose contributions allowed *Bathrooms* to be completed. Heartfelt gratitude to my dear friend, Kevin Clark, who, as always, came through with flying colors. Thanks to my assistant, Julie Maher, and to Celeste Sissons and David Weiss—two well-organized assistants. Much appreciation to my dear friends, Bridget Marmion, for her patient listening, and Jill Cohen, for her belief in this book; to Annetta Hanna, the most patient and insightful editor around, and to Barbara Marks whose genius as a publicist is very much appreciated.

Thanks also go to Deborah Geltman and Gayle Benderoff, my terrific agents, who brought me together once again with all the special and talented people at Clarkson Potter: editorial director Lauren Shakely, whose on-target advice always is sought and appreciated; Michelle Sidrane, a brilliant publisher; all the people in the publicity department, especially Andy Martin, Wendy Schuman, Jennifer Graf, and Chesie Hortenstine; Allison Hanes, an uncommon assistant, who always kept this book on track; Howard Klein, the master of art direction; Maggie Hinders, whose design and layout skills make this book perfect; and Mark McCauslin and Joan Denman, who shepherded the book through production.

As always, I am indebted to the generosity of my friends who opened up their homes and lives to me: Barbara Barry, Friederike and Jeremy Biggs, Jeffrey Bilhuber, Karin Blake and Bill Levine, Laura Bohn, Agnes Bourne and Jim Lubbers, Richard Brayton, Scott Bromley, Vance Burke, Christine Cain, John Clausen, Michael de Santis, Mary Douglas Drysdale, Diane Burns Eden, Steven Ehrlich, Richard Ekstract, Inger McCabe Elliott and Osborne Elliott, Evergreen House, Robert Federighi, Bran Ferren, John Fincher, Lee and Howard Forman, Glenn Gissler, Harold Gordon, Keith and Candy Green, Victoria Hagan, Kitty Hawks, Caroline Hirsch, Benjamin Huntington, Gary Hutton, Arnelle Kase, Noel Jeffrey, Jed Johnson, Gus, Duke Klauck, Dr. Michael and Judith Kraynick, David Duvier Kuehn, Susan Lanier, Joseph Lembo, Pam and Bob Levin, Shaun and Beverly Matthews, Jessica McClintock, Beverly McGuire, Carol Meredith, Andrea and Marc Michaelson, Juan Pablo Molyneux, Charles Morris Mount, David Murdock, Lili Ott, Michael and Bonnie Pappadio, Passanella & Klein, Phyllis Paulson, Christopher Purvis, Andrée Putman, Jann Ramsey, Martin Richards, Jaime Rojo, Nan and Norm Rosenblatt, Barbara Scavullo, Bob Sheffield, Leslie Horan Simon, Paul Siskin, Elizabeth and Jay Smith, Thurston Twigg Smith, Joanne and Richard Stevens, Stephanie Stokes, Henry Stolzman, Susan Stringfellow, Max Wolfe Sturman, Michael Trapp, Lynn von Kersting, Richard Irving, and India, Alan Wanzenberg, Clair Weisz, Vicente Wolf, Peri Wolfman and Charley Gold, and Caroline and Michel Zaleski.

Behind the scenes are friends whose guidance, advice, and direction made this book turn into a reality: Jim and Jennifer D'Auria, Judy Auchincloss, Liz Bruder, Mario Buatta, Sue Masania at Indigo Seas, Stephen Werther at Portico, Lisa Pearl, Stacy Pearl, and April Pearl at Modern Classics, Robert Garrett, Lisl and Dennis Freidrich, and Mike Strohl.

Index